The Provocative Church

———◆———

Third Edition With Study Guide

Graham Tomlin

The Revd Dr Graham Tomlin is Dean of St Mellitus College and Principal of St Paul's Theological Centre, based at Holy Trinity Brompton in London. He worked in a parish in Exeter before becoming Chaplain of Jesus College, Oxford, and then Vice Principal of Wycliffe Hall, Oxford. Among his publications are *The Power of the Cross: Theology and the Death of Christ in Paul, Luther and Pascal* (Paternoster, 1999), *Luther and his World* (Lion, 2002), *Spiritual Fitness: Christian Character in a Consumer Culture* (Continuum, 2006) and *The Seven Deadly Sins and How to Overcome Them* (Lion, 2005). He is married with two children.

To
Janet

———◆———

Published in Great Britain in 2002

Society for Promoting Christian Knowledge
36 Causton Street
London SW1P 4ST

Second edition 2004
Reprinted three times
Third edition 2008

British Library Cataloguing-in-Publication Data
A catalogue record for this book is available from
the British Library

ISBN 978-0-281-06006-1

1 3 5 7 9 10 8 6 4 2

Typeset by Graphicraft Limited, Hong Kong
Printed in Great Britain by
Ashford Colour Press

Produced on paper from sustainable forests

Contents

———◆◆———

Preface

Evangelism and theology haven't always got on terribly well in the past. The common assumption is that if you're an evangelist, you're basically pragmatic and not that interested in theology – it doesn't matter how or why, as long as you get them converted. On the other hand it's assumed that if you're a theologian, then evangelism comes pretty low on your list of priorities. Thankfully this is changing – I keep coming across students and younger Christians who are passionate about evangelism and the desperate need for it in the Church today, yet who also know that if it is to be responsible, to succeed and thrive, it needs a strong theological base.

This book is a contribution to the task of building that foundation. It tries to blend together theology and practice, doctrine and experience.

Martin Luther once wrote that the Church is 'hacked to pieces, marked with scratches, despised, crucified, mocked – like Christ, but to the sight of God, a pure, holy, spotless dove'. The description is probably as true now as in any other time in its past. The obituary of the Church in the West has been written many times, and almost every week new statistics suggest its imminent demise. Yet somehow it survives. Perhaps it's because God loves it. And if God loves it, then the first attitude any Christian must have is to love it too. So, although this book does occasionally offer a critique of the way churches have operated in the past, these are offered in a spirit of love and affection, not hostility.

In one sense this book has taken over 40 years to write. It comes out of long experience of church life, as a child growing up in church, as an involved lay person and subsequently as an ordained minister of the Church of England. Over the years, I've sat through hundreds of services, been heavily involved in at least seven different churches, and known many more through missions, speaking engagements, friends in church leadership and so on. As they say in films, any resemblance between the churches described here and any of these is entirely coincidental!

I have gained and learned more than I can tell from the Christians in the churches I've been privileged to belong to. As anyone who's been involved in one knows, churches can be frustrating, but are often rich and good places to be. They remind me of oysters – not always pretty to look at from the outside, covered in wrinkles and hard edges, but of immense value, because they contain a pearl of priceless value – Jesus himself.

A lot of the ideas here have been written out of my own experience, so perhaps it's best if I explain some of that. I grew up a Baptist, am now an Anglican, and I write with a knowledge of Anglican churches in urban or suburban settings in the forefront of my mind. I still hope some of it will be of use to those in other churches and in other contexts. I've tried not to give a blueprint for what every church must do, but instead to point out some things churches need to think about and work out what they might mean in their patch.

Writing the preface to a book is a little like giving a speech at a wedding – there are always more people to thank than you have time to. Alison Barr and the editorial and production teams at SPCK were very helpful in enabling the book to emerge from my computer into the object you hold in your hands. The ideas were developed in a course taught while I worked at Wycliffe Hall in Oxford, and I'm grateful to all the students who helped refine the ideas, challenged me where I was wrong, made me see new perspectives, and encouraged me to write it down. Wycliffe had a great staff team who were friends as much as colleagues, and students whose passion for Jesus, the Church and for evangelism frequently humbled me. In particular I'd like to thank Geoff Maughan, Andrew Goddard, Peter Walker and Michael Green for stimulating discussions on these themes, and those students who helped it along by their encouragement, criticisms and questions. Several friends read through parts of the manuscript; some (in a real act of sacrifice!) read it all, and I'm very grateful to Simon Featherstone, Phil Ritchie, Andy Buckler, Chris Smith and Simon Downham for their comments. They won't all agree with everything, and are certainly not responsible for it, but I am thankful for such good friends and wise counsellors. I'm also profoundly grateful to Ernesto Lozada-Uzuriaga for his excellent and thought-provoking artwork for the cover of this book, and special thanks to Phil Ritchie for his expert help with and contributions to the Study guide that appears in this edition. Last but certainly not least, I am indebted to and eternally grateful for my wife Janet, and Sam and Sian, who have taught me a great deal about living together and enjoying the life God gives.

CHAPTER 1

Evangelism that works and evangelism that doesn't

————◆————

John Diamond was a journalist for the London *Times*. He died of cancer in March 2001, and became widely known in the UK for a series of penetrating and disarmingly honest articles on his struggles with the disease. Along with his book *C: Because Cowards Get Cancer Too*, these helped many people discover a new approach to dying. Two months before his death, he wrote in characteristically courteous tones about the many Christians who had read his column and e-mailed him with spiritual answers:

> There is no level at which the evangelists and I can engage. They tell me about their spiritual product as if I might not have come across it before . . . as if in 47 years of living in a Christian country I might not yet have stumbled upon the concept of Christ as redeemer . . . They don't seem to understand that I can't force myself to believe what I don't believe. Which is the point at which agnostics usually say 'I only wish I could believe', and I used to say that myself. But I've discovered that it's not true. I'm happy not believing, and that's what the evangelists don't seem to understand.[1]

The words are worth pondering slowly. Sometimes Christians assume that people 'out there' are eager to listen to what the Church has to say. The only problem is

1

learning how to say it louder and more clearly. Yet, over the past few decades, indications suggest that more and more people are exactly like John Diamond. Not hostile to or uninformed about Christianity, often interested in spiritual questions and prepared to face the difficult issues of mortality and meaning. And yet the Church is the last place they would look for answers. With a note of sadness, the journalist Paul Vallely (himself a practising Christian) says: 'For most people today, the Church no longer says anything worthwhile.'

Churches around the country are working hard at turning this around and, slowly but surely, many are finding ways of reaching those outside their walls. Various 'process evangelism' courses, especially Alpha, have proved excellent tools to pick up those people, often on the fringes of church life, who are interested to find out more about Christianity. Yet sometimes it is hard to get people to come on the courses in the first place – people like John Diamond, who are simply 'happy not believing'. What about those who are not particularly interested to find out more? Those who wouldn't choose to come on an Alpha course, even if they were invited to do so? Those whose point is not that they don't believe, but that they don't want to believe? What would provoke them to think the Church had anything worth listening to?

So far, so bleak. However, God is not dead. Nor has he yet given up on the churches in the West, even if it's the ones in places like South East Asia, Africa or South America that are thriving. Despite the well-documented weakness of many of our churches, people still do become Christians today, even from the hard-nosed worlds of the media, journalism and politics. One of the best ways of learning is to listen to people's stories. Another, very different tale perhaps might help us glimpse a way ahead.

Finding Jesus

Derek Draper was a successful political lobbyist who subsequently worked behind the scenes for the Labour government in London. A bout of clubbing, cocaine and Ecstasy tablets, along with a very public scandal about political corruption, led to depression and resignation from his government work. Having been told by therapists that he needed some kind of 'spirituality' to balance his life, and finding yoga, New Age remedies and Buddhism all lacking something, a powerful experience on a visit to Westminster Abbey was followed up by an invitation to his local church, a high Anglican parish with an attractive mixture of the solemn and the informal. The impact is probably best described in his own words:

> I started to discover Jesus Christ, his life and teachings. I'm still learning about the liturgy, and there's no doubt that as I read I struggle both with aspects of the Bible, especially the Old Testament, and with the actions, past and present, of the organized church. What I know, though, is that none of that matters too much. The core of my Christianity is a belief in the wisdom of Jesus' words as told in the Gospels. Now I look back on that time of excess in the mid to late nineties (work, money, drink, drugs, sex, power) with horror. I'm going to try to live my life according to what Jesus laid down 2,000 years ago. I used to live a shallow, materialistic life. I was impatient and intolerant. Now, I try to think and act with others in mind. It's a nauseous idea to

many, but there is no other way of putting it: 'God is love,' says the Bible, and that is what I bear in mind now – love for everyone I meet, unconditional, patient and kind.[2]

Interesting. In fact there are quite a few fascinating things about this account. First, Derek Draper was drawn to the spiritual search by a moment of crisis. Depression and drugs are a potent combination, and usually add up to despair. While he was living his successful political career, high on adrenalin, narcotics and power, Christianity was not remotely even on the horizon. It took something to stop him in his tracks, to make him think again. It's a fairly typical Prodigal Son story, substituting advertising and politics for the far country, and a rehabilitation clinic for the pigsty, but it follows a well-trodden route – through despair to discovery, through sleaze to salvation. Despite affluence, financial security and even the pleasures of family and friends, crises still hit people's lives now as much as they ever did. The questions of why there is life at all, what it means and how it is to be lived have still not gone away, even if the Christian answers seem less obviously true than they used to.

However, cancer too is a moment of crisis and, as John Diamond teaches us, crises on their own don't inevitably lead someone to God. The question is whether and how Christians can offer something at moments of such crisis to open up a viable way ahead, which satisfies the restless soul, and which answers the questions that are being asked, rather than the ones we Christians like answering. This leads us to the second thing: it happened through a church – a provocative church.

We sometimes say these days that people don't tend to drop into churches very often. Maybe it's true. Maybe they don't do it as much as they used to. However, at least Derek Draper did, and the key question was what he found there when he turned up. At that stage his interest in Christianity was on a par with his interest in yoga, Buddhism and ancient Japanese healing. In other words, pretty standard for someone on the spiritual search today. Like many others, he dipped his toe into the water of each of these pools and, naturally enough, was drawn to the one which felt right.

A number of years ago I was given the difficult job of organizing a study day for students in two very different church institutions, without it ending up in theological warfare. I decided to get them all out on the streets, using a basic questionnaire to ask ordinary people about their impression of church. One finding that surprised us all was the very high number of people who had been inside a church within the past year. Whether it was a baptism, a funeral, a wedding, invited by a friend, just dropping in for some peace and quiet, or just trying it out, we were amazed by how many people had drifted in. The other side of the coin, however, was that they had also drifted out. Presumably there was little there to make them want to come back. Derek Draper's church was different. There was something about it which gripped him:

> That Sunday, I walked into a church service for the first time since I was thirteen. I had stumbled upon the perfect church for me . . . the splendour of the robes, the incense and the beautiful choir mixed with an informality that was summed up on All Saints' Day, when two altar boys mounted the steps with day-glo trainers showing under their vestments. That first Sunday, the vicar managed to combine a sermon addressing fear with a genuinely funny joke . . . I was hooked.

The point is not the style of worship – similar stories can be told of less liturgical churches. The point is rather that he sensed something real, different and distinct in the life of that church as they met together: something provocative. It makes us ask a question of any local church – if he had dropped into yours, would it have made him come back for more?

Third, what interests me is the word he uses to describe what attracted him about Jesus: what appealed to him was the practical *wisdom* of the teaching of Jesus. We might have wanted him to come armed with a number of key theological questions, such as 'Where can I find forgiveness for my sins?' or 'Is this logically coherent?' but, doctrinally at least, it wasn't as clearly formed as that and it rarely is.

He was looking not for a guaranteed place in heaven, or guilt forgiven, but quite simply a better and less superficial way of life. It was the prospect of learning a style of life steered by the priority of love, which seemed so much better, richer and more fulfilling than anything he had found elsewhere. It was not so much the ideas and intellectual content of faith that were at issue, but Christianity as a way of life. Christian doctrine and the Bible became valued not primarily because they could be shown to be objectively 'true', but because they were the foundations of a healthier and more rounded existence. Perhaps this shouldn't surprise us, if we know anything about the postmodern condition with its suspicion of truth, or even the Bible and its vision of an incarnate Word, but here was a search for something spiritually satisfying and practically workable.

Douglas Coupland is a perceptive Canadian author, who wrote the book and coined the term 'Generation X' to describe the children of the 1980s, born into affluence and apathy, committed to nothing, laid back and heavily overdosed on irony. In one of his books, *Life after God*, he writes of this generation as the first to have grown up without any sense of God at all – their parents were at least taught the basics of Christianity as they grew up, only to reject it as adults. Now their children are emerging into life after God. Towards the end of the book, the character at the heart of the story, drifting off alone into the wild in search of something almost indefinable, expresses his heartfelt desires:

> Now – here is my secret: I tell it to you with an openness of heart that I doubt I shall ever achieve again, so I pray that you are in a quiet room as you hear these words. My secret is that I need God – that I am sick and can no longer make it alone. I need God to help me give, because I am no longer capable of giving; to help me to be kind, as I no longer seem capable of kindness; to help me to love, as I seem beyond being able to love.[3]

Over the past few years, I have occasionally heard this quotation used by Christian preachers and apologists: at last here is a true postmodern telling us that God is necessary after all. Yet I wonder if the most important thing here is not the fact that he needs God, but the way in which he expresses his need for God. Like Derek Draper, he doesn't sense a need for God to forgive him, teach him the truth, or to satisfy his curiosity about the origins of the universe. Instead, he needs something or someone who can help him learn how to give, to be kind and to love. Now a Christian would want to say that we learn these things by first learning that there is a God who gives to us, who is kind to us, who loves us with a passion far deeper than we can ever fathom. You can never separate Christian doctrine from Christian ethics. Yet the question is framed in this way – he wants to learn these moral qualities, which he knows are essential to human flourishing, and looks for a place where he can learn them. These three lessons put together offer some directions for the way ahead. They tell us that the questions are still there; they tell us that the quality of church life is a vitally important issue for evangelism, and they tell us that if Christian faith can offer a radically different agenda, a distinctive style of life to those available elsewhere, it will have a great appeal to many people. Yet, somehow, we have to come clean, and admit that very often, it isn't working.

The Church and the spiritual search

It's a commonplace in both church and non-church circles to say that despite all the prophecies of wholesale secularization, interest in spirituality and the spiritual search is growing, not declining, today. Buddhism, yoga, meditation techniques, feng shui and New Age therapies are all suddenly respectable, and are all over the Sunday supplements. Religion and spirituality sections of high-street bookshops are far more likely to stock titles such as *The Spiritual Teaching of the Tao* or *The Dalai Lama's Book of Wisdom* than the most recent volumes in Christian theology. Yet the secularists are right in that this spiritual search has not seen a mass return to Christianity. In fact, church is often the last place that people who read such books would look for something truly 'spiritual'. It's estimated that around two-thirds of those who have become seriously involved in New Age-type practices and beliefs have tried church at some time or other, and found it had nothing to offer.[4] Christianity seems part of the old world being left behind, not the new age that is coming.

If there is this large-scale turning towards spirituality, why then has Christianity not seen the benefit? Two broad reasons might be given. On the one hand, there are parts of Christian theology that cut directly across postmodern and New Age concerns. Christians do believe there is such a thing as truth and that it can be found. They believe that there are kinds of behaviour that are objectively right or wrong. And what is more, the Christian faith has always declared that Jesus is the one and only Lord of heaven and earth, a claim most postmoderns would shudder at.

More important perhaps is the second reason, which is that, as Nigel McCulloch puts it, 'the issue that the churches must face up to . . . is not so much that people do not believe in God, but that they do not find the churches credible'.[5] There is something missing, something that a postmodern generation looks for but fails to find in church life. Jean Baudrillard, commenting as he so often does on the way in which postmodern culture is dominated by the surface image, writes some prophetic words: 'None of our societies know how to manage their mourning for the real.'[6] A sense of a lack of depth, a lack of reality, pervades this culture so much that no one quite knows any more what is real and what is fake. For Baudrillard, this nostalgia for reality is one of the key hallmarks of a postmodern world.

Graham Cray, a perceptive commentator on postmodern culture, tells of a student who commented after a presentation of the Christian gospel: 'It doesn't seem real. It seems true, but it doesn't seem real.'

George Monbiot, the author of the influential book *Captive State*, and a key figure in the anti-globalization movement, describes himself as 'not religious'. Yet he speaks for many when he offers his reasons for drifting away from church:

I was brought up with the classic middle-class Anglican stance, which effectively means plenty of form, and very little function, and just a semblance of belief – going through the ritual of going to church on Sunday morning but not allowing your professed belief to interfere in any way with the way you lead your life. It's a very easy ethos to shed, because it isn't really an ethos at all . . . What counts is what churches do, much more than what they profess . . . they must match the positive things they say with action.[7]

Put Baudrillard, the anonymous student and George Monbiot together and again we find another clue to why the churches don't seem to appeal. It's not so much a lack of truth (there are many words in churches, claiming and even demonstrating truth) but a missing connection between the words uttered and the style of life that results from it: a lack of authenticity, of depth, of correlation between words, images and reality.

To put it bluntly, church attendance sometimes doesn't seem to make any great difference to people's lives. If going to church and calling myself a Christian makes almost no discernible difference to the way I live my life, spend my money or use my time, then it is not surprising if my friends who are not Christians are not that interested in finding out any more about it.

One of the key themes of this book is that unless there is something about church, or Christians, or Christian faith that intrigues, provokes or entices, then all the evangelism in the world will fall on deaf ears. If churches cannot convey a sense of 'reality' then all our 'truth' will count for nothing. Unless someone wants to hear, there's no point in shouting louder. Churches need to become provocative, arresting places which make the searcher, the casual visitor, want to come back for more.

Now this might seem just a pragmatic point about supply and demand. However, there is an important theological dimension to it as well. To put it simply, the Christian God can only be found by those who desire him. The point can perhaps best be explained in the words of the great seventeenth-century Christian apologist, Blaise Pascal.

The God of the philosophers and the God of Jesus Christ

Pascal never saw his fortieth birthday. He was an anguished, illness-ridden, often lonely man who, at the cutting edge of contemporary scientific experimentation, felt keenly the intellectual ferment of his times. One November night in 1654, he experienced a profound encounter with God, which turned a distant and arid faith into a gripping sense of mission and devotion. He died eight years later in voluntary poverty, leaving behind scattered papers, probably intended as a grand apology for Christianity. These were subsequently gathered together and published by his friends as the famous *Pensées*: 'Thoughts on religion and various other subjects'.

Among these fragments, two simple points are made again and again. First, Pascal pointed out that because of basic human sinfulness, we only tend to believe what we want to believe. If we don't *want* something to be true, we are remarkably good at thinking of reasons why it isn't. Second, he argued that the Christian God doesn't stand at the end of an argument, ready to be proved, then ticked off as something known and then ignored. He is an intensely passionate God who, when he comes into relationship with people, 'unites himself with them in the depths of their soul . . . and makes them incapable of having any other end but him'.[8] You either have this kind of intimate personal encounter with God, or you don't have him at all. Those who are idly curious, who don't really want this kind of God and are only playing theological games, will not find him. It is only those who hunger for him deep within themselves, who are desperate to know him, who will find what they are looking for.

So, for Pascal, presenting someone with a list of proofs for Christianity or evidence for faith is probably a waste of time. If someone basically doesn't want to believe, no amount of proof (or proof texts) can ever convince her. And even if she were convinced, then it wouldn't be the Christian God she had come to believe in, but only what Pascal called 'the God of the philosophers'. The crucial factor in persuading someone to believe, then, is not to present evidence, but first to awaken a desire for God in them. In other words, when commending Christianity to people, 'Make it attractive, make good men wish it were true, and then show that it is.'[9] Such arguments as there are for Christianity can convince those who hope it is true, but will never convince those who don't.[10]

Pascal would probably have thought that many of our assumptions about evangelism start in the wrong place. I have been on (and even led!) many evangelism training courses that have spent quite a bit of time persuading Christians that they need to know how to answer lots of complicated questions, such as 'Why does God allow suffering?' and 'Don't other religions also lead to God?' Now these are important issues, not least for Christians to work out; after all, they puzzle us sometimes too, not just our non-Christian friends. Or again, evangelism training sometimes focuses on learning a memorable 'gospel presentation' that can be explained to people, often with diagrams drawn on the back of an envelope. In themselves, these are useful things, good for helping Christians to understand the basics of their faith, and sometimes perhaps for explaining it as well. Yet perhaps we need to start a stage further back. It is not just a case of shouting a bit louder, or explaining a bit more articulately. The truth is that it doesn't work like that in the twenty-first century any more than it did in the seventeenth. Pascal's point is that before we ever get to the stage of explaining or convincing, there needs to emerge in people the desire, the question, the hunger to discover more, to find God. Now Pascal, like the great St Augustine before him, was fully aware that only God does that, only God can touch the heart and make it long for himself; yet he also knew that God often uses people like himself and ourselves to awaken that desire.

Creating the desire for God

If all this is anywhere near true, the first stage in a church's approach to its non-Christian neighbours may not be in thinking 'how can we persuade them that it's true?', but by asking 'how can we make them want to know more?' This might involve questions of personal lifestyle: 'How different are my values, my home and my behaviour from those of my neighbours and friends who are not Christians? Is there anything there that might make them want to know more, to want what I have?' It also involves frank and honest questioning of church lifestyle: 'Is our church just another little club for like-minded people who happen to enjoy singing, religious emotion and sermons? Or is there anything in the life or worship of our church that would make an outsider looking in want to have what we have?' An evangelistic lifestyle then becomes one that simply makes other people think. It stirs a faint echo of desire to discover what it is that makes the difference. And this cannot be done alone. To maintain a lifestyle that is different from the culture around is lonely work. It can't be kept going for too long without the strong support and encouragement of a few other people committed to living this way. Derek Draper's story teaches us that when the Church does live by and display a different wisdom, then God can use even something as small as a sermon which helps people conquer fear, or even day-glo trainers, to create the desire for himself.

In other words, a community of people that lives by God's ways, that has learnt to place love, humility, compassion, forgiveness and honesty right at the centre, will make people think. To put it differently, a church that lives its life under the kingdom of God cannot help but provoke questions. And when it does that, then is the time for evangelism. That is the time for the simple explanation of the good news of Jesus Christ.

But that is to get ahead of ourselves. Before we step out on the path of understanding 'how', we need to ask the question 'why'. Why do we do evangelism? Why, in a pluralist, relativist world, would Christians want to make themselves unpopular by forcing their views on others in the first place? Wouldn't it just be easier to keep quiet? These are important questions. The next chapter goes back to basics to try to give some answers.

Notes

1 *The Times Saturday Magazine*, 6 January 2001.
2 *The Times*, 21 February 2001.
3 Douglas Coupland, *Life after God*, London: Simon & Schuster, 1994, p. 359.

4 Nigel McCulloch, *A Gospel to Proclaim*, London: Darton, Longman and Todd, 1992, p. 84.

5 McCulloch, *Gospel*, p. 46.

6 Jean Baudrillard, 'Simulacra and Simulations' in *Modernism/ Postmodernism*, ed. Peter Brooker, London: Longman, 1992, p. 159.

7 George Monbiot, *Third Way*, August 2001, p. 22.

8 Blaise Pascal, *Pensées*, translated by Alban J. Krailsheimer, Penguin Classics, Harmondsworth: Penguin, 1966, p. 169.

9 Pascal, *Pensées*, p. 34.

10 For more on Pascal's Apologetics, see Graham Tomlin, *The Power of the Cross*, Carlisle: Paternoster, 1999, pp. 207–55.

CHAPTER 2

Should we be doing this?

————◦►————

Let's be honest, evangelism is not in fashion. The word 'evangelist' conjures up for many people a slick, oily-haired man in a dark suit and tie, smiling out of a TV screen, Bible in hand, with the phone number for donations at the bottom of the picture. Most evangelists I know are as far removed from this caricature as Brad Pitt is from the Queen of England, but mud sticks. Like it or not, the word carries negative rather than positive overtones for most people outside (and often inside) Christian circles, and the image remains.

However, it's not just that evangelists are seen as seductive manipulators with a secret agenda of grabbing your cash. A deeper unease, endemic in contemporary Western societies, is felt towards anyone who thinks they have the truth, particularly those who want to persuade you of their truth. Laid-back, playfully cynical postmoderns find evangelists just a bit tiresome as they bang on about the virtues of their brand of religion, when everyone knows that no one brand is any better than any other. More strident liberals are afraid that Christians, given half a chance, could be every bit as zealous for their certainties as radical Islamists are about theirs. Basically, it's far more hip to be uncommitted, keeping a safe ironic distance between yourself and commitment to any particular world view. Or at least if you do opt for a particular brand from the smorgasbord of early twenty-first-century faith options, you certainly shouldn't try to force your views on anyone else.

16

Should we be doing this?

Postmodernism could be defined (to misquote Jean-François Lyotard) as 'incredulity towards evangelists'.[1] Those with a gospel to proclaim, with certainties, confidence and grand propositions which claim to be true in an ultimate sense, are precisely the kind of people that postmodern people distrust. The prevailing culture seems to give a pretty clear message, at least as far as religion goes: if it's OK for you, then fine, but don't push it on me.

The historical roots of this position are tangled, yet the broad lines are clear. After the religious wars of the sixteenth and seventeenth centuries, and under the banner of 'Enlightenment', European intellectuals questioned the role and necessity of supernatural, revealed religion within Western society. If religion was to survive it would have to be in a bastardized form, stripped of any claims to divine revelation, miraculous features and a truth beyond reason.

Before long, Hume was questioning the self-evident existence of God, Rousseau was arguing for a society based on rights not responsibilities, and Kant proposed ethics deriving from human not divine sources. Enlightenment thinkers and their successors mounted a vigorous, sustained and historically successful attack on all the distinctive features of Christianity – including the uniqueness of Jesus Christ, and the authority and inspiration of the Bible – and proposed its reinterpretation as a moral code with a pale Galilean Jesus and a distant God. The Enlightenment dreamed of a society that somehow retained a strict moralism (despite the demise of divine commands), human reason as the ultimate arbiter of truth, and the strict elimination of the spiritual and supernatural as explanations of anything important.

If that was the basis of what is often called 'modernism', then its offspring – 'postmodernism' – has pulled the rug from under the feet of its own parent by extending the same critique to the Enlightenment's own cherished beliefs. Whereas the Enlightenment replaced the authority of Bible or Church with that of reason, postmodernism replied that this vaunted 'reason' was nothing like as objective and impartial as the Enlightenment thinkers had believed. Instead, it was simply a collection of assumptions by middle-aged white imperialist men, who foisted their opinions on everyone else. It was no more objectively 'true' than Christianity was. For example, it seemed self-evidently 'rational' to eighteenth- and nineteenth-century men that the Western way of life was best and that the light of Western European trade and custom should surely transplant sullen heathenism. It now no longer seems such a good idea. Now not only Christianity and reason itself but every other grand story claiming to give a total understanding of the whole of life has endured the same treatment, including the Enlightenment's other children, idealism, Marxism and Fascism.

The result is a belief in nothing or, perhaps more accurately, as G. K. Chesterton pointed out, a belief in everything. There is no overarching 'truth' that everyone must believe, yet the range of options of lifestyle choices and belief systems is dazzling, so that I can gaze at New Age crystals at the same time as working out in health and fitness clubs, arrange my home according to the principles of feng shui, go clubbing at nights and engage in Buddhist meditation when I wake up in the morning. Christianity takes its place among these as just another private lifestyle choice. And of course this is fine, just so long as you don't try to force it on anyone else.

At the same time, modernism itself is making a comeback. Reborn rationalists such as Richard Dawkins and Daniel Dennett argue against what they perceive as the irrationality of faith and the evils religion has foisted upon the world. They want a return to good old Enlightenment certainties – the certainties supposedly offered by science, and definitely not those of religion.

So how can evangelism operate under such conditions, where one great sin is to think you are right, and the other is to believe in something you can't prove? And what is the role of the Church in such a culture? Does it have a role? Is it any more than a religious version of the Rotary Club, or a harmless collection of coffee mornings, a pleasant diversion from the harshness of a brutal world?

It has to be admitted that sometimes evangelism has been done for less than helpful reasons. We try not to run violent crusades any more, but even still, some of the militaristic language and aggressive behaviour of some modern evangelism skirts dangerously close. Similarly, evangelism that seems to consist mainly of warning everyone in sight that they are destined for hell not only chooses a negative motivation that Jesus usually reserved for religious hypocrites, but also introduces an unhelpful measure of emotional and spiritual tension into any discussion, making dialogue pretty difficult.

Yet we need to ask whether evangelism has any place in a pluralist, postmodern society where racial and religious tension is never far from the surface and if so, what that place might be. What is the Church meant to be in days like ours? When it comes to evangelism – should we be doing this at all? And if so, why? What's needed is some basic orientation – a map for the journey, which will help us see the lie of the land. And perhaps the best way to find our way around is by asking a wise and reliable guide.

The Church between the world and the kingdom

Jacques Ellul was one of the most perceptive Christian commentators on Church and society in the twentieth century. Born in 1912 and dying in 1994, he was a professor in the Law Faculty at Bordeaux University in France, lived through two world wars, the beginnings of the information revolution and most of the vast social changes which the last century saw. Throughout that time he was active in the French Reformed Church. In 1948 he published a book that many see as the key to the rest of his work, and that has some prophetic and provocative things to say about the place of the Church in Western society. It was called *The Presence of the Kingdom*.[2] Although written more than half a century ago, it still speaks powerfully with foresight and understanding, and can perhaps help us as we try to find the place of the Church and evangelism within a new century.[3]

Ellul insists that the Christian has no option but to live in the world. It may be an obvious point, but his warning is directed on the one hand at those who prefer to retreat into some private cosy religious sphere, and those at the other extreme who think they can succeed in creating a Christian society. The Christian is caught uncomfortably between these two impossible options, and Ellul goes on to suggest some vital attitudes Christians need as they relate to the world around them.

Christians need to try to understand the true character of the world they live in, and not be deceived into thinking that really everything is just fine, Ellul suggests. Just as the Old Testament prophets repeatedly warned against social complacency, so contemporary Christians too are to look beneath the surface and understand what really drives society along. We live in societies where the gap between poverty and wealth gets wider every year and where the three richest billionaires in the world have more assets than the combined wealth of the 600 million people of the world's least developed countries. In our world, violence is a normal way of getting one's own way in both personal and international disputes, children are frequently abused by adults who view them as objects for their own pleasure or ambition, and countless people are unable to sustain long-term relationships and so marriages fail acrimoniously. From global warming to daily pollution of rivers and the encroachment of cities and superstores into green spaces, the environment in so many places is being consumed and destroyed, and the sustainable resources of the earth are being used up with little thought for the future. In both large and small ways, people are regularly treated as objects to be exploited rather than precious creations to be treasured.

It's a pretty bleak picture, and Ellul, like many a prophet before him, has been accused of being overly pessimistic. Yet he insists on naming the demons – these factors are present and arguably growing in Western societies. Of course good things happen too: love, mercy and justice do occasionally triumph. Yet the reality that pervades the world – what Christians call sin and evil – must be faced and identified.

Second, Ellul argues, Christians need to question the way the world is. In other words, they must refuse to accept that the way things are is the way they always will be. Abuse, environmental decay and loveless self-indulgence may dominate many people's lives and the general drift of society, but it need not always be like this. Things could be different. These do not have the last word, and should not be accepted as inevitable 'facts of life'. There is another, a better way, and even if it is hard to see it in this age, yet still the Christian holds on to the hope of that better way.

Third, Christians must realize that the world needs nothing less than a revolution. Ellul means this not in the Marxist sense of changing the government, and installing a different set of sinners – that doesn't really make a great deal of difference. It means recognizing that the world as it is presently run is a pretty destructive place. It is destructive of relationships, of people, of peace, and of justice. Children and adults are abused, either in dramatic criminal acts, or in routine, ordinary ways, and rarely do we find ourselves treated as the extraordinary beings we are, created in the image of God with dignity and a huge capacity for joy. Tinkering with the present system may introduce minor improvements, but the Bible calls for something much more radical: the full appearance of the kingdom of God, a new age in which Christ's victory over sin and death will have its full effect.

Having painted the landscape that Christians find themselves in, Ellul then goes on to outline proper ways of living and reacting in such a place. First, the Christian's role in such a society is as a sign of a different kingdom, a different way of life. Writing of the Christian in the world, he says:

> Of course he can always immerse himself in good works, and pour out his energy in religious or social activities, but all this will have no meaning unless he is fulfilling the only mission with which he has been charged by Jesus Christ, which is first of all to be a sign.[4]

Christians are not meant just to try to do good, be nice and help the world work a little bit better. They are instead to act as signposts to another order, another way of life, another kingdom, which can be glimpsed in this world, but has not yet arrived completely. Ellul warns us against thinking that this kingdom can be established entirely here and now under current conditions. It is *God* who builds his kingdom and will bring it into being – it is not for us to do this. However, those who believe in God's kingdom and kingship will want to act as signs of that kingdom, offering reminders, aromas, tastes of what it might mean to live under God's rule, not the iron law of sin and death.

Following on from this, Ellul insists that the Church's identity is more important than its function. In other words, what we *are* is more important than what we *do*. The most urgent task Christians face in the present is to develop a distinctive 'style of life' that expresses the life of this other kingdom. It's worth quoting Ellul at some length here, to get a picture of what he is trying to say:

> In order that Christianity today may have a point of contact with the world, it is less important to have theories about economic and political questions, or even to take up a definite political and economic position, than it is to create a new style of life . . . Fidelity (to revelation) can only become a reality in daily life through the creation of this new way of life: this is the 'missing link'. There used to be a style of life peculiar to the Middle Ages. In the sixteenth century, there was a style of life carried on by Reformed Church Christians, and it is extremely interesting to note where it was opposed to the style of life of the Renaissance. There is a bourgeois style of life, which has no spiritual quality at all; there is the Communist style of life; there is no longer a Christian style of life. To speak quite frankly, without beating about the bush, a doctrine only has power

(apart from that which God gives it) to the extent in which it is adopted, believed, and accepted by men who have a style of life which is in harmony with it . . . The whole of life is concerned in this search. It includes the way we think about present political questions, as well as our way of practicing hospitality. It also affects the way we dress and the food we eat . . . as well as the way in which we manage our financial affairs. It includes being faithful to one's wife as well as being accessible to one's neighbor . . . Absolutely everything, the smallest details we regard as indifferent, ought to be questioned, placed in the light of faith, examined from the point of view of the glory of God. It is on this condition that, in the church, we might possibly discover a new style of Christian life, voluntary and true.[5]

Ellul puts his finger on what many feel is the long-term weakness of the Church in the West – a failure to live in any distinctive or alternative way to the ways of life on offer in the wider culture, despite all our theological expertise and liturgical correctness. Ellul suggests that the rediscovery of a genuinely Christian way of life (rather than just getting our doctrine right) is the key to the re-birth of Christianity in the West. It reminds us of Derek Draper's need for a practical wisdom to live by. Such wisdom will mean living as if it really is true that this planet is made and loved by a creator God; that each person we meet is a precious being, crafted in God's own image, to be treated with dignity and reverence; that God's judgement on a sinful world is real and imminent; that sin and death are now empty, broken forces since the death and resurrection of Jesus; and that one day God will bring in his new kingdom of justice, peace and joy. A life that assumed these realities would look very different from a life that knows nothing of them.

Finally, Ellul insists that this must be done *together*. The task of forming a new, genuinely Christian way of life that acts as a sign of the kingdom to come can only be done in community. Again, Ellul speaks best in his own words:

> It is impossible for an isolated Christian to follow this path . . . In order to undertake this search for a new style of life, every Christian ought to feel and know that they are supported by others . . . It will be necessary to engage in a work that aims at re-building parish life, at discovering Christian community, so that people may learn afresh what the fruit of the Spirit is . . . We shall need to rediscover the concrete application of self-control, liberty, unity, and so on. All this is essential for the life of the church, and the function of Christianity in the world. And all this ought to be directed toward the preaching and the proclamation of the gospel.[6]

Ellul envisages small, mutually supportive communities of Christians committed to living out of the Christian story, discovering what it means to live under the rule of God in a secular and sometimes hostile world. These are places in which Christians find the help they need in working out how to live as a Christian businessperson, office worker, shop assistant, solicitor or engineer, and find the solidarity and practical support needed when it gets pretty tough trying to do just that. Ellul sees in all this a vital role for lay Christians. He criticizes both clergy who are out of touch with the real world because they don't participate in it, and lay people who are careful to keep their faith and their 'ordinary lives' in quite separate compartments. He's also deeply suspicious of a type of spirituality that withdraws faith into an inner sphere of religious feelings, and that has no outward practical and social expression at all. For him, Christian laity have a central role as they, not the clergy, are the ones living day by day on the edges of the 'two cities', to borrow Augustine's language, the City of God and the City of the World.

As we start to think about evangelism in the contemporary world, Jacques Ellul reminds us of the importance of three crucial things that will be close to the heart of this book – the kingdom of God, developing a way of life that reflects that kingdom, and the importance of local church communities in this very task.

Evangelism and revolution

Ellul did not explore in any great detail the implications of this for evangelism. Another guide to help us make this connection is the Old Testament scholar Walter Brueggemann, and in particular a small but stimulating book published in 1993, called *Biblical Perspectives on Evangelism*. Brueggemann argues that if you are a Christian, the story that tells you who you are is not the story of your parents, ancestors, ethnic group or social class. It is instead, the story of the Bible – the *promise* to Abraham, *deliverance* from slavery to Egypt and sin, and the *gift* of land to landless Israelites and life to dead sinners. This story of promise, deliverance and gift is your family history, the story that defines you. In short, you are lovingly created, redeemed, and transformed; you belong to the God of Jesus Christ. Now this story is of course very different from the stories that define many other people's lives. There, the story might tell of the despair of a single mother struggling to bring up a child on her own, the boredom of a middle-aged executive who has all the comfort modern life brings but no purpose or meaning, or the deprivation of a child born into poverty, living under disadvantage and exclusion.

Brueggemann then defines evangelism as 'the invitation to reimagine our lives . . . an invitation and summons to "switch stories" and therefore to change lives'.[7] It is the invitation to exchange the gods of despair, boredom or disadvantage for the God of Jesus Christ – a God of promise, rescue and generosity. Jacques Ellul summons Christians not to give in to the tired old stories of the world around them, not to assume that things can never be any different. Brueggemann takes this further, by encouraging us to see evangelism as an invitation to move from this tired world to the new age, the new kingdom of life under the reign of God, which challenges the harsh rule of other gods. Like Ellul, his is a call to a new imagination – refusing to believe that the chains of despair, boredom or deprivation are unbreakable and daring to let one's imagination roam – to believe that there is another way, another king.

In one of Bruce Chatwin's fine haunting books, *The Songlines*, an Irish priest is asked his opinion of another brilliant but enigmatic character in the story: 'Flynn has to be some kind of genius . . . but I don't think he was ever a Believer. He could never take the leap into faith. Didn't have the imagination for it.'[8] It's a perceptive and telling verdict. Faith needs imagination – the ability to imagine that things could be different, that what you see is not necessarily what you get.

Both Ellul and Brueggemann help us see that the beginnings of Christian life and witness lie in dissatisfaction with the way things are. A sense that 'things should not be like this' is the true beginning of wisdom. For St

Paul, one of the signs that the Spirit of God has begun to work in a person is that we 'groan inwardly as we wait eagerly for our adoption as sons, the redemption of our bodies' (Romans 8.23). Frustration is one of the lesser-known fruits of the Spirit! Dissatisfaction with the way things are, accompanied by a deep instinct that things could be different, are the starting points for anyone who wants to engage with the God of Jesus Christ.

Evangelism in a modern and postmodern world

To return to our original question, these insights about the kingdom of God offering a different way and opening up new possibilities are also a useful starting point for anyone wanting to engage in evangelism in a modern and postmodern age. Perhaps a familiar story will help explain this point a little more clearly.

The legend of Robin Hood is well known – the one who stole from the rich to give to the poor, who lived in Sherwood Forest with his merry men and Maid Marian, and regularly managed to annoy the Sheriff of Nottingham. What relationship the story bears to historical reality is hard to tell. However, the context in which the story is usually set is significant. In the twelfth century England's rightful king, Richard, had left the country to fight in the Crusades. In his absence, his brother Prince John had set himself up as king in his place. Not content with this, John had also inflicted heavy taxation on and curtailed the hunting rights of the peasants, who were already kept firmly in their place by a strict feudal system. Robin Hood was the leader of a kind of resistance movement that refused to accept the rule of 'King' John, and kept alive the hope of the return of the true king,

Richard. When news began to filter through to England that King Richard was on his way home, and had in fact landed, Robin Hood and his followers began to whisper the news around to their fellow countrymen, who had by now given up hope, that the true king had not forgotten, that things were going to be different. For a while they still had to live under uncertainty and even oppression until 'King' John was finally defeated, but the news was out, and nothing could keep them quiet.

Robin Hood's band of resistance fighters is perhaps a surprising, but not a bad image for the Church in the world today. They live under an oppressive regime, but they can smile and laugh because they know that the present system is not the last word. They know that the true king is coming, and that things will one day be different. From time to time, they still remind the false powers that their rule is temporary and bogus, by acts of rebellion that recall the true king. They also whisper around the good news that things don't have to be like this. The king is coming, in fact he has already landed, and others can begin to live joyfully in the light of this coming kingdom as well.

This is essentially what evangelism is – the simple announcement that there is another king, another kingdom that will one day become fully visible, and the invitation to take part in it. It also explains why Christians evangelize, even under apparently hostile conditions. Postmodernity may or may not have succeeded modernity, depending on who you talk to, yet both have harsh and cruel climates. As so often, it is the secular critics who can see what Christians sometimes cannot. Terry Eagleton, for example, in speaking of 'the appalling mess which is the contemporary world',[9] unmasks postmodernism:

29

. . . a scepticism of totalities, left or right, is usually fairly bogus. It generally turns out to mean a suspicion of certain kinds of totality, and an enthusiastic endorsement of others. Some kinds of totality – prisons, patriarchy, the body, absolutist political orders – would be acceptable topics of conversation, while others – modes of production, social formations, doctrinal systems – would be silently censored.[10]

Whether in classical, medieval, modern or postmodern times, the most striking thing is history's 'remarkable consistency – namely the stubborn persisting realities of wretchedness and exploitation'.[11]

The world could be different, yet, contrary to the socialist dream of critics like Eagleton, the Christian despairs of human attempts to make it better. Only divine action, the full coming of the kingdom, can make a difference. Why do we evangelize? Because things could and should be better than they are. Our present way of life is not the only way of life. And because we have heard news that there is another king, another kingdom, under whose rule things are very different. And here is the good news – the kingdom *has* come, in Jesus Christ. The king has arrived and you can see signs around that things are becoming different.

Now to some, this may seem far too 'this-worldly'. Surely evangelism is about saving souls for eternity? Surely it's about ensuring that as many people get to heaven as possible? We'll look in more detail at what Jesus means by the kingdom soon. In the meantime, it's worth remembering, however, that the Bible talks about saving people, not souls. The idea that we are saved as disembodied souls destined for a vague heaven up and

30

out there somewhere is perhaps more of a Platonic Greek myth than a biblical idea. The Bible speaks of the goal of salvation being a 'new heavens and a new earth'; it speaks of the resurrection of the body, not just the soul; it speaks ultimately of heaven coming down to earth as a sovereign act of God, not of us vanishing off to heaven. This present world order, the rule of sin and death and hell will be overturned, to be sure, but that doesn't mean the destruction of the earth and our soaring off to some spiritual theme park in the sky – the Bible assures us that God will transform, not destroy, the earth; he will transform, not destroy, our humanity.

We sometimes think of the kingdom of God as a place people go when they die, maybe a vague spiritual world somewhere far removed from this earth, and as a consequence, the normal stuff of life that we live day by day doesn't seem to matter a great deal compared with the task of getting people ready for heaven. But is this really what Jesus meant by the kingdom of God? Does hope in the future kingdom mean this world is of no real significance? These are questions which the next chapter will look at much more closely.

In the meantime, the king has established a beachhead in enemy territory. Jesus has come, and inaugurated the kingdom. And perhaps most importantly, he has made it clear that this is a kingdom of joy, celebration and – not to be too precious about it – of fun. The images Jesus used to describe the kingdom were always full of delight. It is like a feast with lavish food and great hilarity, or a woman finding a priceless lost necklace and throwing a party to celebrate. The picture of a bunch of outlaws celebrating with huge joyful meals deep in the forest in defiance of the false powers is the same kind of story. This is no stern, solemn king, exercising a humourless, cold rule. It is the rule of a gracious host, inviting us into his home, the place where he is in charge, and where there is lots of rich, deep laughter. Miserable, gloomy and dull churches have simply missed the point. Churches who have truly grasped this are communities where there is a great deal of enjoyment. And their joy rests on much stronger foundations than any on offer elsewhere. On deeper inspection, the breathless search for a 'good time' can so often seem like thin laughter only briefly masking the final realities of evil and death. Joy that is built on the coming rule of the true king, full of goodness, warmth and welcome, is far richer.

So the Church's place and role in contemporary societies, as it is in any society, is as a sign of the true kingdom. And evangelism has a place as the announcement, not of a disembodied and philosophical truth to be debated, but of an actual state of affairs. It is good news, not good ideas. It announces not an abstract set of concepts, but a reality that can be glimpsed and experienced – life under the rule of the true king. Perhaps we can begin to see, however, that this means rethinking evangelism, or at least setting it into a much larger context than perhaps we are used to. In the next couple of chapters, we begin to address that task. We have touched on important theological themes such as the lordship of Christ, and the kingdom of God. These have their roots in the New Testament, and so it is there that we must go to explore what this kingdom means, and how it relates to the task of evangelism today.

Notes

1 Lyotard of course famously described the postmodern condition as 'incredulity towards metanarratives' in Jean-François Lyotard, *La Condition Postmoderne: Rapport sur le Savoir*, Paris: Editions de Minuit, 1979, p. 7.

2 Jacques Ellul, *The Presence of the Kingdom*, 2nd ed., Colorado Springs, CO: Helmers & Howard, 1989. (Original French version: *Présence au monde moderne*, 1948.)

3 I am indebted to my colleague Dr Andrew Goddard, whose book on Ellul (*Living the Word, Resisting the World*, Carlisle: Paternoster, 2002) is a useful introduction, and provides a development of some of the ideas presented here.

4 Ellul, *Presence*, p. 5.

5 Ellul, *Presence*, pp. 119–23.

6 Ellul, *Presence*, pp. 123–4.

7 Walter Brueggemann, *Biblical Perspectives on Evangelism: Living in a Three-Storied Universe*, Nashville, TN: Abingdon Press, 1993, pp. 10–11.

8 Bruce Chatwin, *The Songlines*, London: Picador, 1987, p. 72.

9 Terry Eagleton, *The Illusions of Postmodernism*, Oxford: Blackwell, 1996, p. ix.

10 Eagleton, *Illusions*, p. 11.

11 Eagleton, *Illusions*, p. 51.

CHAPTER 3

The king, the kingdom and the Book

————◆————

When the first three Gospel writers put pen to papyrus, they knew exactly what they had to write about. As they painted their pictures of Jesus of Nazareth, this remarkable man who had literally changed their world, one theme had to be emphasized above all others, simply because it had been the main theme on the lips of Jesus himself. It was the announcement of the kingdom of God.

It is hard to get New Testament scholars to agree about much but most concur that Jesus' teaching and ministry focused upon the kingdom of God. Mark's Gospel opens with the voices of Isaiah and John the Baptist echoing in the desert. In fulfilment, Jesus then strides onto the stage from the hills of Galilee. The introduction reaches its climax when Jesus, given divine approval during his baptism by John, finally opens his mouth to proclaim: 'The time has come. The kingdom of God is near. Repent and believe the good news!' (Mark 1.15). It's a dramatic opening, and is as good a summary of Jesus' message as you can get.

Jesus told parables mainly it seems to explain what the kingdom of God was like.[1] The kingdom was 'near', it was 'coming' in power, it was like a mustard seed, a merchant seeking pearls, a king preparing a banquet for his son, a farmer planting crops, a woman baking bread with yeast. It may not always be easy to pin it down to a neat formula, but at least there's no mistaking how central it was to Jesus' idea of his role in the complex unfolding of Israel's history.

However, it's one thing to agree that the kingdom of God was central for Jesus; it's another to identify exactly what it was.[2] To begin to do that, it's vital to go back well beyond Jesus himself. Like most things on the lips of Jesus, the kingdom was not an idea he dreamt up out of thin air. It had a long and complex history in Israel's past. It had shaped the heart and the hopes of the nation Jesus belonged to, and can't be understood outside of that context.

When Jesus entered the last few very public years of his life, Israel had for a long time been waiting for God's kingdom to come. However, when they mentioned this hope, first-century Jews weren't looking for the end of history nor life after death. Instead, the 'kingdom of God' was quite clearly a very down-to-earth political idea. Centuries before, the nation of Israel, once a significant presence in the Near East under the great kings David and Solomon, had become divided, and then endured the further shame of exile in Assyria and Babylon. Although groups of Jews had dribbled back into the land since the Babylonian King Cyrus had unexpectedly allowed them to leave in 538 BC, the greatness had vanished. The slowly rebuilt Jerusalem lacked the grandeur of the past, and a hastily constructed new temple was a pale imitation of the great and glittering edifice Solomon had erected. By the time of Jesus, these disappointed hopes had intensified under occupation by another foreign power, imperial Rome. Even though Herod the Great had now built a new and impressive temple, Yahweh's own land was still occupied territory, and the people waited for release. In the minds of most Jews of Jesus' time, the exile was still not over. When they hoped for the kingdom of God, they were looking for God himself to become king again over his own land, his own people, and ultimately over all the nations. As Tom Wright puts it, the kingdom of God 'was simply a Jewish way of talking about Israel's God becoming king'.[3]

At the time of Jesus, many questions reverberated around the nation. Why was God taking so long about it? What would happen when he did decide to act? How could Israel help to bring it about? Different groups took different lines on these sensitive and highly charged questions. The priestly Sadducees, the party that held the reins of power, believed that maintaining temple worship was the key factor. For them, continued sacrifice in the temple was the condition of Yahweh's return. Another group, the Essenes, thought this grand new temple in Jerusalem, built by the half-caste King Herod the Great, was a sham, and its sacrifices an insult to the God of Israel. So, they withdrew to the desert shores of the Dead Sea, just 15 or so miles away from Jerusalem, where they waited for God to act decisively, overcoming the sons of darkness, and vindicating them as the only remnant of Israel who had remained faithful. The Pharisees were less radical, remaining within the mainstream of Jewish life, yet insisting on Israel's national and ritual purity as the incentive that would encourage God to act. The Zealots took a more hard-line approach. Waiting for God to act on his own was pointless. Acts of rebellion were called for, popular uprisings that would throw off the yoke of God's enemies and restore Israel to its rightful place, and put God back on his throne.

Despite these different methods, most of these shared the same hope – that the kingdom of God would come. They also recognized the same reality – that it had not yet done so. Onto this stage came a young rabbi, emerging from the Galilean shadows, announcing to anyone who wanted to listen that the kingdom of God was actually here; that God was now acting at last to restore his rule in the world. Not surprisingly, he generated some excited interest, as well as a touch of scepticism. Jesus' programme, however, was quite different from those of the Sadducees, Essenes, Pharisees or Zealots. To grasp what it was, we need to go back to some key Old Testament texts that kept alive the hopes of the kingdom, as they were read again and again in synagogues and temple, and see what happens to these themes in the life and words of Jesus.

The kingship of God in the Old Testament

In the eleventh century BC, Israel finally got a king, just like all the other nations. Although Saul himself proved something of a disappointment, the reign of his successor, the great King David, saw the kingdom of Israel reaching its peak. The next king, Solomon, even built a proper temple to serve as the house of God in Jerusalem. But from there on, according to the biblical writers, it had all been downhill. Weak rulers created shameful scandals, and the whole thing ended in civil war and the shame of exile. The Psalms, a book of prayers and songs used in Solomon's temple, celebrated good kingship over and over again. Just read Psalm 99 sometime to feel the awesome festivity of the temple worship as it swayed between declaring that 'The Lord reigns – let the nations tremble', and marvelling that in David they have a ruler who is just like God – 'the King is mighty – he loves justice'.

In David's heyday, however, there was a feeling that even this era, great as it was, was only a foretaste of something better. In 2 Samuel 7, at the height of his powers, we find David dissatisfied even with his success, and so deciding to build Yahweh a house, more like his own palace, and certainly better than the shabby tent reserved as God's dwelling place at the time. Yet Yahweh has other ideas. Through David's prophet Nathan, Yahweh declares that David will not build him a house; rather he will build a house for David:

> When your days are over and you rest with your fathers, I will raise up your offspring to succeed you, who will come from your own body, and I will establish his kingdom. He is the one who will build a house for my Name, and I will establish the throne of his kingdom for ever. I will be his father, and he shall be my son. When he does wrong, I will punish him with the rod of men, with floggings inflicted by men. But my love will never be taken away from him, as I took it away from Saul, whom I removed from before you. Your house and your kingdom shall endure for ever before me; your throne shall be established for ever. (2 Samuel 7.12–16)

One day, a king would appear from among David's descendants, who would build the temple or house for God that David wanted to build, and whose kingdom would be established for ever.

With that in mind, we turn to what happens towards the end of Jesus' life, especially as Mark tells the story (Mark 11.9–18). Followed by his nervous disciples, Jesus moves towards the climax of his mission as he walks down from Galilee, passes the Essene commune at Qumran (did they come out to watch?), and turns to climb the gradual ascent from the Jordan plain up to Jerusalem, past the bare hills where the Zealots hid.

When he arrives in the capital, Mark records three distinct episodes involving a colt, a fig tree and the temple. When I heard these stories explained as a child, I somehow got the impression that they were there to show Jesus' amazing powers. Wasn't it great that Jesus just *knew* somehow that there would be a donkey ready for him? Just look at Jesus – he only has to say a word and a tree shrivels up! It was as if Jesus was flexing his divine muscles to show what he really could do, right here before the big crowds in the capital. Yet that is entirely to miss the point.

Mark wants us to know that all three actions were carefully thought out and meticulously planned. They were not chance reactions to unexpected events, but deliberately symbolic actions, each with its own meaning – they were, in fact, acted parables.

Jesus and Jerusalem

If I was near Washington DC, and wanted to get to the city centre, I would go by bus. I would not hire a limousine, place on it a prominent presidential flag and arrange to be driven in, surrounded by an ostentatious motorcade. Yet this is pretty much what Jesus did when he arrived in his capital city. Jesus chose to enter Jerusalem this way not because he was suddenly overcome with a fit of weariness and caught a lift on a passing donkey. Mark lets us know that Jesus had made plans for there to be a colt ready for him, even giving the disciples the right code-word to give to its owner. Everyone knew the prophecy of Zechariah, that when God's king finally came to Jerusalem, he would come 'riding on a donkey, on a colt, the foal of a donkey' (Zechariah 9.9). That's exactly why no one in their right mind would enter the city this way – it would be exactly like hiring a

39

presidential limousine to drive into the capital, which is pretty crazy, unless that is, you are the President.[4]

The crowd of course, knew exactly what Jesus was saying, as they applauded his arrival with just the right words: 'Blessed is the coming kingdom of our father David!' (Mark 11.10).

So, here is Jesus, laying deliberate claim to be the Son of David, the king that Jerusalem has been waiting for all these years. Here was God's king, coming to take up his throne in God's city among God's people. With all that Jesus had already said about God's kingdom coming, this was it. Here was the king about to be enthroned in his own capital city.

Jesus and the fig tree

So, what about the fig tree? Was Jesus suddenly struck with pangs of hunger? Looking around for something to eat, did he get angry with a hapless fig tree for failing to provide it, then curse it in a fit of temper? Unlikely. Again, Mark is at pains to remind us that Jesus knew it was not the right time of year. He was not stupid, and was no more surprised by the absence of figs than we would be to see a barren apple tree in winter. Here again, the Old Testament background is vital. In an agricultural society where each family tended their own orchards, the withered fig tree was a frequent and vivid symbol of divine judgement on Israel.[5] Here was an acted parable, saying something hard to hear and unlikely to make Jesus many friends – the moment of judgement was coming. Israel's king was coming to look for fruit and, finding none, the nation would be made barren. Jesus' own people Israel were now to come under Yahweh's judgement for refusing to acknowledge her true king.

Jesus and the temple

Finally, Jesus performs the most provocative act so far. At Passover time, while the city is heaving with people and tense with expectation, Jesus strides up the steps into the temple courtyard, stands in the way of anyone trying to use the temple as a short cut, chases out some of those selling sacrificial animals and scatters the tables of the men changing foreign currency into Jewish coins. For a short while, he effectively halts the normal business of the temple. After delivering a concise, punchy speech, he leaves, and the demonstration is over as quickly as it had begun, giving the authorities little time to react. Most scholars today agree that Jesus was eventually crucified because of this brief but aggressive act.[6] Yet what exactly did it all mean?

The title normally given to this incident, the 'Cleansing of the Temple', implies that Jesus' main concern was to clean it up from some kind of defilement, restoring purity to a holy religious site. Was Jesus mounting a protest against the use of filthy lucre in a holy place? Coming into the temple, was he consumed with a holy rage at seeing commerce in a place of prayer, and out of zeal for God did he banish corrupt merchants from the sanctuary?

Again, unlikely. Even this is clearly planned. To eliminate any idea that this took Jesus by surprise, Mark says that Jesus entered the magnificent building on his first evening in Jerusalem, and had a good look around before retiring to Bethany for the night. As a good Jewish pilgrim, he had been to the temple many times before and knew exactly what was there. Moneychangers in the temple courtyard were no great shock, even if their stalls were a relatively recent addition to the temple furniture.

He, like all Jews, knew the whole point of the temple was sacrifice – that is what it was there for. And if you wanted sacrifice, you had to have animals, vegetables or incense to offer in sacrifice. The temple rules decreed that sacrificial offerings had to be bought with a special currency – Tyrian shekels. As a result, every pilgrim wanting to offer sacrifice had to exchange their own money for this special temple coinage. Moneychangers were therefore an integral and necessary part of the whole system. Moreover, there is no suggestion anywhere that they were particularly corrupt. Something else is going on.

The temple lay at the very heart of Israel's political and religious life. Still today, religious Jews gather daily to pray and study Torah at the Western Wall in Jerusalem, as close as they will allow themselves to the ancient Holy of Holies. More extremist Jewish groups occasionally utter dark threats to destroy the Muslim Dome of the Rock and the Al-Aqsa mosque, which stand today on the old temple site, and build a new third temple on the site, an action that would be high on the list of those most likely to spark a third world war. The violent conflict which ravaged Israel from the late 1990s was sparked by two seemingly innocuous events – the opening of a door under the Temple Mount and the visit of an Israeli politician to the site itself. Still today, this is a place that ignites conflict and seethes with tension.

In Jesus' day the temple was just as potent a symbol and just as controversial. It was a vast building, set in a rectangular courtyard covering about 500 × 300 metres on the site of Solomon's previous temple, about one sixth of the city's area. Out of all the places on earth, this hill, called Mount Zion, was where God had chosen to dwell (see for example Psalm 87; 132.13–18). It was the place where daily sacrifices were offered for the sins of the people, for thanksgiving and worship. It was also the symbol of Israel's uniqueness and distinctness from all the other nations – after all, no other city had the true temple of God in its midst.

When we imagine religious places, we perhaps think of vast cathedrals, hushed reverence, people walking on tiptoes and speaking in whispers. The temple in Jerusalem was entirely different. This was a noisy, energetic place. There was shouting, bartering, animated discussions, and at the centre where the sacrifices took place, blood-spattered walls and the foul stench of dead animals under the Eastern sun.

Around the edge of the temple area was a covered portico where animals could be bought for sacrifice, and Greek or Roman currency changed into Tyrian shekels. Inside that was a large open courtyard, where anyone could mingle. At the centre rose the temple itself, entered by a door through which only Jews could go – Gentiles were excluded from this point in. Inside this door lay the Court of the Women, so called because this was as far as women were allowed in the temple structure. Beyond this courtyard lay the crowded Court of the Israelites, where only Jewish men could enter. Beyond this still lay a further area into which only priests could pass, and then finally, at the very centre of the whole edifice, was the Holy of Holies itself, into which only the high priest could enter, once a year to burn incense on the Day of Atonement. (See Figure 3.1.)

In other words, the entire temple structure was built around the principle of exclusion and, at successive points, Gentiles, women, non-priests and then even the priests themselves were excluded, leaving the high priest himself as the only one allowed to enter the holiest place of all. The original idea had been to emphasize God's holiness; the unintended effect had been to encourage Israel's separateness.

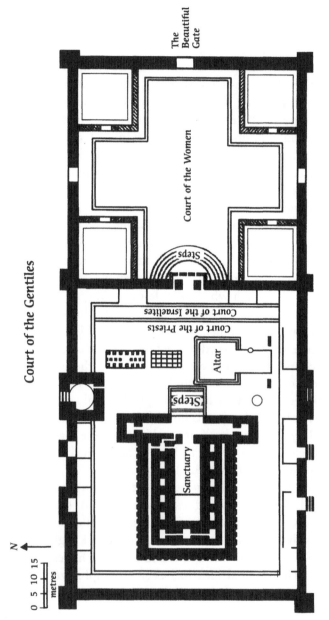

Figure 3.1 The temple in Jerusalem in Jesus' day

The Beautiful Gate

Court of the Women

Steps

Court of the Gentiles

Court of the Israelites

Court of the Priests

Altar

Steps

Sanctuary

N

0 5 10 15
metres

Against this background, the words Jesus utters during his brief demonstration in the temple make a great deal of sense. He quotes directly from Isaiah's prophecy that the Gentiles will find a place in God's temple (Isaiah 56.7), and Jeremiah's famous protest against the temple of his day (Jeremiah 7.1–11). Jesus' complaint is precisely that the temple was intended as a 'house of prayer *for all nations*'; adding 'but you have made it "a den of robbers" ' (Mark 11.17). In other words, the very architecture of the building, standing at the heart of Israel's religion, run by the nationalistic and powerful priestly caste, had become an unintentional symbol of the nation's exclusivity. A people who were meant to be a 'light to the Gentiles', bringing salvation to the ends of the earth (Isaiah 49.6), had become centred upon their own separateness from those very Gentiles. Their only concern was maintaining their own purity, their own ethnic boundaries, keeping strangers out rather than welcoming them in. The temple had become a symbol of resistance to the Gentiles rather than their inclusion in God's kingdom.[7]

Jesus' protest against the temple was a public statement against the nationalism that had crept into Israel's soul.[8] The temple had become the symbol of Jewish ethnocentricity and therefore its hopes for survival. As long as the temple stood, so they thought, then all was well – it was the guarantee of security, just as it had been in Jeremiah's day, just before the disaster of exile and destruction. For Jesus, exactly the same was happening now. Whether it was the Sadducean route of temple worship, the Essene route of withdrawal, the Pharisaic route of national and religious purity or, more acutely, the Zealot path of armed rebellion against Rome, all of these agendas centred upon national identity and separateness. None of them were God's way. The 'robbers' living in the den of the temple were not in fact the moneychangers but rather they were the 'chief priests and the teachers of the law' – the custodians of temple worship and of Israel's religious life, who had stolen what was intended for all peoples and kept it for themselves. They knew Jesus' action was directed at them, and it's not surprising that it is they, not the moneychangers, who at the end of Mark's account (Mark 11.18) begin harbouring murderous thoughts towards him.

It's worth stressing of course that Jesus' condemnation of Israel was by no means anti-Semitic. It was precisely out of love for the nation, loyalty to Israel's God and horror at what had become of God's chosen people that he acted out his mission of judgement and delivered his invitation to join the coming kingdom of God. This was just what the great Old Testament prophets had done. It was not anti-Jewish polemic; it was inter-Jewish debate. Nonetheless, Jesus' message was stark: for those who understood its meaning this acted parable, in line with those enacted by the prophets of Israel's past, was a prediction that this temple would soon be destroyed, which is of course exactly what happened when the temple fell to Roman battering rams, catapults and cavalry in AD 70.

Jesus had come to Jerusalem as the Son of David, God's king. It was even rumoured that he claimed to be able to rebuild the temple,[9] something which only David's promised king could do.[10] The days of this temple were nearly over. The time had come for a completely new kind of temple. Now the Gentiles were to be brought into God's people, as had always been expected when God set up his rule on earth. Now was the time when, as the prophet Joel had predicted, God would dwell on earth not in a specific location, but among his people.[11] All that the temple offered, the presence of God himself, forgiveness and reconciliation with God, the central point of God's chosen people, was now to be found not in a building in Jerusalem, but in the person of Jesus himself.[12] Jesus was the king who would build the true temple, the place where God dwelt, in his own person, and in those who decided to follow him. The reception Jesus received showed starkly that God's king had come to take his throne, to claim what was his own, but had been firmly rejected.

The coming of the Son of Man

As a young theology student, when I came to study the New Testament, one passage seemed to come up again and again as I read books on the background to Jesus' life. It came in the book of Daniel, and contained a strange vision, described by a Jewish writer many centuries before. In the vision, he saw a great mysterious figure, God himself, the 'Ancient of Days', dressed in dazzling white sitting on a throne of fire. Then there appeared another figure, this time a human one:

> In my vision at night I looked, and there before me was one like a son of man, coming with the clouds of heaven. He approached the Ancient of Days and was led into his presence. He was given authority, glory and sovereign power; all peoples, nations and men of every language worshipped him. His dominion is an everlasting dominion that will not pass away, and his kingdom is one that will never be destroyed. (Daniel 7.13–14)

Later on, I began to notice how intriguingly similar Matthew's account of the climax of Jesus' life sounds. At his trial, Jesus, who of course has referred to himself throughout by this same title 'Son of Man', predicts that his enemies will 'see the Son of Man sitting at the right hand of the Mighty One and coming on the clouds of heaven' – just like in Daniel's story (Matthew 26.64). Not surprisingly, the high priest is outraged – he knows his Old Testament well enough to know what Jesus is saying. In the final words of Matthew's account, Jesus leaves the disciples. As he comes before God, he too is given 'all authority in heaven and on earth', and because of this, his followers are to 'go and make disciples of all nations' (Matthew 28.16–20).

The echoes are unmistakable and deliberate. Yet in Matthew's version of the story, two big changes are made. First, it is Jesus, not Israel, who is given God's authority and kingdom. He is the one who rules on God's behalf over the nations of the earth. The Son of Man, who now possesses all authority in heaven and earth, is not the nation of Israel, as most first-century Jews would have expected, but Jesus himself.

Second, the enthronement is delayed. In Daniel, the Son of Man takes up his position of authority right away. In Matthew, Jesus receives kingship and authority, but until the 'end of the age' (28.20), his kingship is to be demonstrated through the making of disciples who are learning to obey everything Jesus has commanded. The meaning of this present time, before the end of the age, is therefore the time when Jesus' authority over the world (which is God's authority, given to him) is to be preached, lived, demonstrated and learnt. All nations and peoples are to be invited under his rule, to acknowledge his claim to be God's true king. His followers are to make disciples of all nations because he is the true king who deserves the allegiance of all those nations. He is the Lord of heaven and earth, the one Daniel dreamt about, in whom God's rule has come.

The kingdom and the gospel

Jesus' ministry climaxed in the most unexpected of ways. He was enthroned as king, but on a cross, not a throne. He did defeat the enemies of God and his people, but they turned out not to be the Romans, but the powers of sin, death and hell, which were overcome through his death on the cross. His claim to be God's king was vindicated, not by popular acclaim, but by divine recognition, as he was raised from death to sit at the right hand of God in glory.[13] Jesus became the Lord of heaven and earth, but his kingdom was unlike any other found on the earth. The Jews in Thessalonica got it just right when they complained to the city officials: 'They are all defying Caesar's decrees, saying that there is another king, one called Jesus' (Acts 17.7). This is, in essence, the good news of the gospel: that Jesus Christ has come as God's king, and that his enemies and the enemies of humankind have been dealt a fatal blow from which they will never recover. Or to put it in the three-word summary that the early Christians gave to sum up their message: Jesus is Lord.

Jesus offered healing, forgiveness, reconciliation with God, an open community, feasting and a renewed and a rebuilt temple. All of these were signs that Israel's exile was over; they were all signs that God's kingship had come near at last. Where you find these things, you know that God is in charge. It did not mean that the world was transformed overnight, but that here, in this one person, God was establishing his kingship again on earth. And in the subsequent gift of the Spirit of Jesus there came the possibility that members of his community could begin to act and become like him.

The next chapter will explore in more detail what all this means for evangelism and the Church, but as this one closes, it's time to sketch out some of the contours of the kingdom which Jesus came to bring.

1 *This kingdom is open to all peoples.* Jesus picked a fight with the Judaism of his day because of its pre-occupation with nationalism. Israel had forgotten her calling to be a 'light to the Gentiles', the bearer of God's message to the ends of the earth. Unlike the temple, the kingdom Jesus spoke about was to embrace Jew and Gentile, men and women, priest and non-priest. It was open to all peoples, nations, races and genders.

2 *This kingdom is different.* When Jesus chose to enter Jerusalem on a colt, this was a sure sign that his was to be a kingdom of peace. While other contemporary agendas were aggressive and militaristic, in Jesus' kingdom (in the words of Zechariah) chariots and war-horses would be banished, 'the battle-bow will be broken' and peace would be announced to the Gentiles (Zechariah 9.10). Not only is his kingdom different, but Jesus also becomes king in a startling way. His throne is a cross and his crown is woven out of thorns. Jesus is proclaimed 'King of the Jews' only when he is hammered onto a Roman cross.

This is a king like no other. In his kingdom, a very different set of values reign. This kingdom is not recognizable by the usual marks of human rule: ostentatious power, wealth and status. Instead, this kingdom is marked by the presence of meekness, mercy, poverty, purity of heart, generosity, kindness, love and forgiveness. Its central symbol is a meal where people from all corners of the earth will be invited to sit down together in delight and welcome.[14] If the words 'kingdom' and 'rule' carry a heavy authoritarian tone in our postmodern world, suspicious of all power and hegemony, then that says more about our bad government than it does about God's strong and gentle reign. When they come from Jesus' lips we have to learn a different meaning to these words, pointing us to the rule and kingdom of love, mercy and joy, not power and oppression. To be a member of this kingdom means learning a whole new set of values, a different way of life.

3 *The kingdom is demonstrated by actions.* It's sometimes said that the heart of Jesus' ministry lay in his teaching, and that his actions (for example, his miracles and the kind of acted parables we've looked at here) were secondary, almost a distraction from the teaching. Actually, the reverse is true. Jesus came not primarily to teach some new ideas, but to bring in the kingdom of God. His words are in fact a commentary on what is happening in his actions. They explain the significance of what is taking place as he heals the sick, raises the dead, walks on water, confronts the temple and goes to his death. These were the signs that the kingdom of God was drawing near, that the exile was now over, that God had come to rule again. Jesus' teaching draws out the significance of these actions and helps those who have ears to hear to realize their significance. This will have important implications for our understanding of the relationship between words and actions in evangelism, but we'll come on to that in time.

4 *Recognition of the true king means rejection of other kings.* Jesus' announcement of the kingdom was not primarily an invitation to life after death, or an inner spiritual journey (although it included both of these). It had clear material and earthly implications. It's not that Jesus wasn't offering a path to the full presence of God after this life, yet in the first instance, the kingdom

meant changes and revised priorities and loyalties here and now. It meant living now in the light of the fact that the kingdom had come in part, and one day would come in its fullness. Loyalty to Jesus as God's king meant learning a way of life that echoed his character and style. It meant rejecting the lordship of other claimants to that title. Herod the Great may have thought he was 'King of the Jews', but followers of Jesus could never give him that honour. Caesar may have called himself 'Lord', but again, followers of Jesus would have to resist that claim. Jesus alone was Lord, and his ways must be followed. There was therefore a distinctly political, material and controversial character to Jesus' bringing of the kingdom of God. If he is God's king, there can be no other.

Just as Jesus' message was revolutionary in its time, his announcement of the kingdom also has some revolutionary things to say to us about evangelism in the local church today. The next chapter begins to draw some of these out.

Notes

1 For example, Matthew 18.23; 22.2; Mark 4.26, 30; Luke 13.18.
2 Naturally in a short chapter like this there is no room for an exhaustive treatment of such a key topic. For recent scholarship, readers are referred to books such as George R. Beasley-Murray, *Jesus and the Kingdom of God*, Grand Rapids, MI: Eerdmans, 1986; Bruce Chilton, *Pure Kingdom: Jesus' Vision of God*, Grand Rapids, MI: Eerdmans, 1996; Wendell Willis (ed.), *The Kingdom of God in Twentieth-Century Interpretation*, Peabody, MA: Hendrickson, 1987; N. T. Wright, *Jesus and the Victory of God*, London: SPCK, 1996.
3 N. T. Wright, *Jesus and the Victory of God*, p. 203.

4 Zechariah was probably referring to the promise to David in 2 Samuel 7. Zechariah 9.10 quotes directly from Psalm 72.8, one of the psalms that most explicitly picked up the promise of an everlasting kingdom to the Davidic line. Zechariah's chapter promised that 'never again will an oppressor overrun my people, for now I am keeping watch'. As Jesus entered Jerusalem under the shadow of the imposing Antonia Fortress, the symbol of Roman control towering over the northern edge of the temple itself, his actions could only have been interpreted as implying that God was now becoming king of Israel once again.

5 For example, Isaiah 34.4; Jeremiah 5.17; 8.13; Hosea 2.12; Joel 1.12; Amos 4.9.

6 For example, E. P. Sanders, *Jesus and Judaism*, London: SCM, 1985, pp. 61–71. In Mark 14.58, Jesus is specifically charged at his trial with having threatened the destruction of the temple.

7 See Marcus J. Borg, *Jesus: Conflict, Holiness and Politics*, New York, NY: Edwin Mellen, 1984, pp. 175–7.

8 See Wright, *Jesus*, ch. 9, and Peter W. L. Walker, *Jesus and the Holy City: New Testament Perspectives on Jerusalem*, Grand Rapids, MI: Eerdmans, 1996, p. 277.

9 Mark 14.58, also John 2.19.

10 See 2 Samuel 7.13.

11 Ezekiel 36.26; Joel 2.28–29.

12 Wright, *Jesus*, p. 436.

13 Matthew 26.64 and parallels; Acts 2.33.

14 See, for example, Matthew 8.11; Luke 13.29; 14.15–24.

CHAPTER 4

The kingdom, the Church and evangelism

————◆————

Jesus came to launch the kingdom; he ended up with the Church. It doesn't sound a very good deal. Did he intend to found the Church? Was it all a big mistake, a game of Chinese whispers that went badly wrong? It's still argued about today, but there is a good deal of evidence to suggest that even if Jesus didn't envisage cathedrals and synods, he did envisage small communities of people committed to living out his vision of the kingdom, and continuing beyond his life on earth.

For a start, the fact that he chose twelve disciples to correspond with the twelve tribes of Israel suggests pretty conclusively that he thought of his small band of followers as a newly reconstituted Israel. His practice of table-fellowship with his followers culminating in the new Passover meal, where he shared bread and wine with them on the eve of his death, again indicates the same kind of idea. It would surely be odd for Jesus to begin this new vision of Israel without imagining that in some way it would continue after his death. Jesus probably envisaged small cells of followers meeting in the towns and villages of Israel, living out the way of life he had taught, centred upon loyalty to himself, mutual forgiveness and love, forgoing the option of armed resistance to the Romans, and taking a radically different approach to the crisis of the times from that of the Zealots, Pharisees, Sadducees and Essenes.[1]

It's intriguing to wonder what Jesus would have thought of the great Church that emerged over the following centuries. It certainly seems very different from the kind of small groups he may have had in mind. We've spent quite some time looking at Jesus' announcement of the kingdom of God, and its climax at the end of his life as he comes to Jerusalem as its true king to experience rejection and finally vindication. The next step is to ask what this means for the Church – in other words, the vital question of how church and kingdom relate to one another, and what this says about evangelism. Moving on from the particular circumstances of Jesus' ministry, it's now time to draw some threads out of the discussion in the previous chapter. With apologies to Martin Luther, the rest of this chapter proposes ten theses (not 95, you'll be glad to hear) on what all this might mean for the Church, the kingdom, the gospel and evangelism.

1 The gospel centres on the lordship of Christ

Get a dozen Christians together and ask them what is the core of the good news, and you'll probably get a dozen different answers. Much emotional and theological energy is spent trying to define the heart of the gospel. However, it is (and should be) possible to give a coherent answer to this question. If what we've seen already is anywhere near true, and Jesus' ministry centred upon the coming of the kingdom of God in his own person, then perhaps the early Christians got it right when they summarized the heart of the gospel with the pithy catchphrase, 'Jesus is Lord'.[2] Jesus is God's king over the world, he has defeated the powers that oppose both God and humanity. He is the one who has the final word. He holds ultimate power, not presidents or prime ministers, guilt or grief, disease or death.[3]

True, themes such as the atonement, the incarnation and the Holy Spirit are vital parts of the texture of Christian theology. Yet if we want to find the heart of the proclamation, the lordship of Christ fits the bill both historically and theologically, and other doctrines fit around it.

For example, the doctrine of the cross as the means of forgiveness fits well into this framework: how can rebels against Christ's lordship be pardoned and acquitted? Forgiveness is not cheap, and rebels can become true and valued citizens only if someone pays the price of forgiveness. The atonement provides the answer – 'Christ died for sins once for all, the righteous for the unrighteous, to bring you to God' (1 Peter 3.18). The same is true for the doctrine of the Holy Spirit: how can failing, disfigured people become those who enact the life of the kingdom as Jesus did, living effectively under Christ's lordship? Only by being filled with the Spirit of Jesus and 'being transformed into his likeness with ever-increasing glory, which comes from the Lord, who is the Spirit' (2 Corinthians 3.18). The incarnation also: how does this 'Lord' Jesus relate to the one and only true 'Lord', the God of Israel whose chosen king he is? The incarnation provides the answer, insisting that in Jesus we see not just as near to God as a human being can get, but a perfect image of God himself, in some sense sharing the very nature of God (more on this later!). Even in this brief sketch we can begin to see how Christian theology can be focused around this central Christian assertion: Jesus is Lord!

For centuries the Church has operated in a culture where the existence and reality of God was unquestioned. In the Middle Ages, for example, most Europeans had no real doubt that God existed, that he saw everything they did and that he would judge their lives after death. The key question was therefore how you might get past this judgement or, more technically, how you might be put right or 'justified' before this God. It's no surprise then that at the time of the Reformation the question of how justification takes place took centre stage in the debates. Luther's point was not so much that justification is central to Christian life and theology – in a sense everyone knew that already. It was more that justification happens by *faith*, simply trusting God's promise of pardon, rather than by generating a real sorrow for sins, trying hard to love God or doing good religious works.

Nowadays, the Church in the West lives in a culture where the idea of God as judge is fast vanishing. That is no longer the framework in which most people think. If they do believe in God, as of course many still do, he is normally considered to be a genial parental figure, perhaps a bit remote from real life, but who will forgive decent people because, as Heinrich Heine once said, that's his job. As a result, perhaps the first thing Christians need to say today is not so much the message of justification, but the message of the kingship or kingdom of God. Before being told how they can be reconciled to God, people need to know who this God is in the first place, the creator of heaven and earth, who generously provides everything for life, who loves his creation passionately, who hates all that is evil and will one day destroy it, and in whom we find true life, joy and peace. It is not that justification has become less important; it's that in a changing cultural setting, we need to start in a different place if we are to proclaim and demonstrate the gospel.

The response to the gospel is of course always the same wherever you go. It may take different forms in practice, but underneath, the same two factors are always present: repentance and faith. This was what Jesus called for – 'The kingdom of God is near. Repent and believe the good news!' (Mark 1.15) – as well as the apostles – 'I have declared to both Jews and Greeks that they must turn to God in repentance and have faith in our Lord Jesus' (Acts 20.21). When a person grasps the good news that Jesus is Lord of heaven and earth, there can be no other response but to repent of living as if that were not true, and starting to believe it and live as if it is.

2 Church and kingdom are not the same

This is fundamental. The late medieval Church made this mistake, allowing itself to entertain far too big ideas about itself, and forgetting that the Church never quite approximates to the kingdom. As a result it began to try to wield political and military power alongside its spiritual authority, and before long needed a deep-rooted reformation to restore some sanity. If church and kingdom were identical, church would be a place where people *always* found forgiveness, love, mercy, healing and justice. I occasionally glimpse these things in church, perhaps even a little more than I do in the rest of society, but no church could realistically claim to have got it exactly right.

The distinction between church and kingdom is very, very important. It keeps the Church humble and understated, and is a healthy corrective to the triumphalism that so easily creeps into any institution that believes that in some way it has a special role to play in God's plans. However, that doesn't mean they have nothing to do with each other. In fact, if Jesus' ministry was focused upon the kingdom of God – which he believed was being established on earth through his own life, death and resurrection – and if he intended his followers to continue to meet around that agenda, then the Church's relationship to the kingdom must be pretty important. In fact, it's surprising that over the years, when the Church has explained and proclaimed its gospel, the kingdom of God has not exactly featured very high in the topics covered.

3 The community of Jesus has the task of bearing witness to his rightful rule

If Jesus' ministry is the story of God's king coming to claim his throne, and establish the kingdom, then the Church exists to remind the rest of the world that that Jesus is God's chosen king, that he has now triumphed over all the powers that diminish and enslave his creation, and that his kingdom is now here to be acknowledged. Surrounded by people, societies and ideologies that do not recognize it, the Church has been handed the task of bearing witness to the lordship of Christ, or the rule of God.

This doesn't mean some kind of imperialistic crusade to force reluctant and superficial allegiance to a new ruler – God (and I mean God) forbid! Instead, it runs much deeper than that. Loyalty to and faith in Jesus as Lord means living in the light of his victory over sin and death and evil, living the way of life Jesus proclaimed, the way of the kingdom values expressed in texts such as the Sermon on the Mount, and embodied in his own person and conduct. This is how human life was meant to be lived, and to this all people are to be invited.

4 The Church is to be a visible reminder of life under God's rule

To take this a stage further, the chief way in which the Church is to bear witness to the gentle rule of God is by being an effective reminder of life under that rule. The new reality brought about by Jesus, where the powers of sin and death and hell are overcome, is to be demonstrated by a community that learns to live as if that is true, and in doing so finds that it *is* true. Churches are meant to be places where people can begin to understand and feel and experience what life is like under God's rule, what a community might look like that really lived in Jesus' kingdom. Lesslie Newbigin asks the pertinent question:

> How is it possible that the gospel should be credible, that people should come to believe that the power which has the last word in human affairs is represented by a man hanging on a cross? I am suggesting that the only answer, the only hermeneutic of the gospel, is a congregation of men and women who believe it and live by it.[4]

What he means is that the only way in which the gospel can be interpreted in terms that make sense to people outside it is when it is lived out in an actual group of Christians in a particular place. Perhaps churches need to be less like the socially respectable and conformist places they have sometimes come to be, and more like the small revolutionary cells that Jesus envisaged he would leave behind in the towns of first-century Palestine. They are to be communities that live by Jesus' vision of the kingdom of God, focused on loyalty to him and the way of life he laid out for his followers. As a result, for those looking in from the outside, they are to be provocative reminders of Jesus' kingdom.

Jerusalem's temple in Jesus' day was rejected because it had kept its doors closed to the nations. The time had now come for it to be replaced by Jesus as the true temple, the place where God dwelt. Jesus came to bring near a kingdom that is open to all, and in which he takes centre stage. This means that churches have to work hard at keeping Jesus at the centre, and the doors wide open. That, as anyone who's ever been remotely near a church will know, is far from easy. In church, we have learnt habits for years that keep the doors firmly closed to anyone different, by subtle tones of our own subculture, or just by a frosty welcome. The last thing some churches want is for anyone new to join, because it might mean change to well-established patterns and long-loved practice. Churches are also remarkably good at edging Jesus out of the centre, and replacing him almost imperceptibly with something else, whether doctrinal correctness, unwritten customs or liturgical niceties.

In every capital city, you can usually find communities of exiles. Chinese restaurants in San Francisco's Chinatown, Turkish restaurants in London, Arab neighbourhoods in Paris. In all of them, communities try to recreate the atmosphere of home, so that when you step inside you can begin to feel what it is like to be in the real country itself. There will be reminders that you aren't actually there yet. The weather in Paris is not always as warm as Saudi Arabia, London Turkish neighbourhoods still have road signs in English. However, these communities remind you of the real thing. They are also fairly good images of what church is meant to be – a community that reminds others of the real thing, the kingdom of God – life under the rule of Christ. There will be reminders that this is not yet complete. Petty jealousies, envy and pride still rear their heads, yet the idea is that church is meant, as far as it can, to be a reminder of life under the rule of God.

5 The Church is to announce the kingship of God

In the last chapter, we saw how Jesus' actions took precedence over his words. This is not to minimize the importance of Jesus' teaching; quite the contrary – it is to give it its proper significance. The Pharisees were troubled by Jesus' ability to cast out demons; after all, he didn't observe the ritual purity they thought was essential to being God's people. In reply, Jesus explains exactly what his exorcisms mean: 'If I drive out demons by the Spirit of God, then the kingdom of God has come upon you' (Matthew 12.28). Jesus' words were a commentary on his actions, effectively explaining to his contemporaries what these signs meant – they were the unmistakable signs that the kingdom of God had finally come upon them.

If this is the pattern of the kingdom, and the Church is called to be like the kingdom, then we might expect the same pattern to operate in the Church. In other words, while the Church is called to be a visible and tangible reminder of life in the kingdom, it can never be enough simply to enact the kingdom, to be a silent reminder that non-members appreciate but do not understand. Just as Jesus' words explained the significance of his actions, then the Church's words have to do the same. If belief in the victory of God over all his enemies in the death and resurrection of Christ has given the community of Jesus' followers unexpected hope, then it must also, in the words of 1 Peter, 'be prepared to give an answer to everyone who asks you to give the reason for the hope that you have' (1 Peter 3.15). Without actions, no one listens; without words, no one understands.

The Church is to remind the rest of the world of God's rule and Christ's lordship in its words as well as its life.

And this means not only commenting upon what's happening in the Church. To repeat, churches are not identical with the kingdom, nor are they the only places where it can be found. Justice, love, mercy, forgiveness and meekness are often found outside the Church, and wherever these things are discovered, there is a taste, a savour of God's rule. Yet as Jesus said to his immediate followers, 'The secret of the kingdom of God has been given to *you*' (Mark 4.11); in other words, it is only the followers of Jesus who know the true meaning of these things, that they are signs that God is still in charge over the earth. Despite the evil regime that has occupied the land, the rumour of the true king survives.

6 Evangelism involves words

Especially since the upsurge in interest in evangelism since the Decade of Evangelism in the 1990s, it has become fashionable to widen the definition of evangelism to include anything that points to God or the Church. I remember reading of a bishop in the Church of England who said that whatever we do for the Church is part of evangelism, so that even mowing the church lawn could be included within its definition. I think I know what he meant and, yes, mowing church lawns, clearing church drains and making church buildings look cared-for and attractive is vital work – they can even become a sign of the kingdom of God. Yet we shouldn't confuse these with evangelism.

Again we are back with the distinction between Jesus' actions which demonstrated that the kingdom of God had come, and the words that explained those actions. As we'll see, evangelism cannot thrive for long without such actions, but they are not the same thing. If we widen the definition of any word to make it mean almost anything, it ends up meaning nothing. Far better, if we want to stick to more traditional terminology on these things, is to define the actions that demonstrate or recall God's rule over the world as 'mission', and the words that explain those actions as 'evangelism'. This seems much more in harmony with the New Testament usage of the Greek word *euangelizomai*, which always seems to bear a verbal content.[5] There is a popular phrase usually attributed to St Francis, which goes something like: 'Travel everywhere, preach the gospel, use words if you have to.' This may say something significant about the importance of good deeds as an inseparable adjunct to evangelism, but unhelpfully confuses the two. As a *definition* of evangelism it's ultimately misleading and theologically unhelpful.

7 The Church exists to invite people to come under the rule of God

In fact this is perhaps as good a definition of evangelism as we can get. At least it will be the definition we'll be working with for the rest of this book. Announcing the kingdom involves inviting people to become part of it. This isn't strictly the same as inviting people to join the Church, but is closely connected to it. Becoming a follower of Jesus means nailing one's colours to the mast of Jesus and his agenda for human life and society. It means acknowledging his rightful rule over not only my own life but over the whole world, and beginning to live as if that is true. At the same time, it isn't unrelated to the Church, the community of the king, the people called to bear witness to and enact the kingdom. It's theoretically conceivable, but doesn't make a lot of sense, to be a member of the kingdom, yet not a member of the community of the kingdom.

Evangelism therefore entails an invitation to come under God's rule, and learn its ways. Just as when a person moves to another country, and has to learn its different laws, language, culture, history and customs, becoming a Christian means entering a new world. It means repenting of my failure to acknowledge God's rightful rule over the world. It means rejecting any other claim to control or wield ultimate authority in the world. It means believing that in Jesus Christ, God has set up his rule on earth and, through the cross, has made forgiveness for that rejection possible, so that the kingdom of God is open even to rebels and sinners like me. It means enjoying the benefits of life under God's just and gentle rule. It means learning the language and values of that kingdom, accepting the discipline and change involved in bringing our lives under God's rule. It means acknowledging God as king and Jesus as Lord both of my own life and of the whole of creation. It means learning to treat others with the dignity they deserve as precious children, made in the image of God. Along with the rest of the community of Jesus, it involves showing the rest of the world what life looks like under God's rule, what a society could look like, how the environment is treated and how people are valued when God is in charge.

8 Evangelism lies at the heart of the Church's identity

Evangelism, the verbal invitation to bring a person's own life under the rule of God, must lie at the heart of the Church's existence. If the good news – that despite appearances God is really in charge of his world, and has established his kingdom in Jesus – is to be preached and lived until the end of the age, then the issuing of the invitation to acknowledge that rule can never be relegated to the back-burner, or delegated to a sub-committee of the church council or deacons' meeting. This is what the Church is there for.

As the last chapter demonstrated, this new kingdom is defined by its openness to all peoples. The moment Israel interpreted its election as a calling to privileged isolation, it became unfaithful to its God, the God of the whole earth. It was as if they had just another tribal god like all the others. The minute the Church becomes a club for like-minded people, enjoying vertical privileges and failing to hold out the horizontal invitation to become a disciple of the king, a member of the kingdom, then it too will lose its identity and direction.

Evangelism therefore arises out of the very heart of the God who established his kingship over the world in the person of Jesus, and who invites his rebellious creation back, forgiven and cleansed to enjoy life under this rule again. If it arises from the very heart of God, it must lie at the heart of his Church. Once that has been fully grasped, it does solve a lot of problems about church life, but we'll come on to that later.

9 Evangelism can never stand alone

If evangelism is understood as 'inviting people to come under the rule of God', then even though we have described it as central to the life of the Church, it can never become the *only* task of the Church. The Church has to be involved in bearing witness to God's rule in Christ, demonstrating what that looks like, showing what human life and community are like when they are lived under God's rule.

Sometimes, churches that have grasped the central place of evangelism within the Church make it the number one priority of the community. The next step is often the fatal one: because it is a central priority, and because resources are limited, it becomes the *only* priority for the church. As a result, pastoral care, worship and practical action in the local and wider community are left on one side as less important than evangelism. These churches often end up as breathless, exhausting places to belong to. Church members are constantly exhorted to personal evangelism, and those members of the congregation who struggle with life, don't have particularly strong evangelistic gifts or who are plagued with doubt are made to feel inadequate.

The priority for the Church is neither evangelism nor social action; it is to live under the lordship of Christ. In other words, the central thing is not a human task, but a divine action. It is not our work of spreading the gospel or changing society, but it is the new reality brought into being by the coming of Christ. Lesslie Newbigin puts it well:

> Because Jesus has met and mastered the powers that enslave the world, because he now sits at God's right hand, and because there has been given to those who believe a real foretaste, pledge, *arrabon* of the kingdom, namely the mighty Spirit of God, the third person of the Trinity, therefore this new reality, this new presence creates a moment of crisis wherever it appears. It provokes questions which call for answers and which, if the true answer is not accepted, lead to false answers. This happens where there is a community whose members are deeply rooted in Christ as their absolute Lord and Saviour.[6]

This is not at all to put evangelism in the shade, or to suggest that it is unimportant – at the very least that would contradict Thesis 8 above! Again, it is to place it in its proper context. As we'll see in the next few chapters, without this priority of life under the rule of God, without the demonstration of kingdom life, evangelism simply doesn't work.

10 The kingdom speaks to the culture

Cultural relevance is not the be-all and end-all of Christian evangelism. However, as any missionary worth their salt knows, if Christians are going to communicate with people around them, they need to speak their language and enter into their mindset. If it's increasingly true that we are living in a culture that has begun to distrust the authoritative voices of the past, then that has to be taken into account. The feature of that culture that concerns us here is the nature of truth.

As we have already seen, contemporary culture in the West (and far beyond if the prophets of globalization are right) has become very wary of disembodied truth. Where truth is suspected of being a mere front for power games, what lies beneath the surface of truth becomes a critical issue. In other words, the connection between a truth claim, and the kind of living that emerges from it, comes under very close scrutiny. Is this truth just another bid for power and mastery over others, just like Fascism and Marxism were, the discredited ideologies of the twentieth century? Evangelism that proclaims a gospel of truth, yet pays little attention to the kind of community it creates or the quality of life of the people it shapes, is unlikely to be listened to for very long by those who have imbibed the postmodern suspicion of disembodied truth with their mothers' milk.

The fact is, however, that Christianity is just as suspicious of disembodied truth. Its truth is always embodied – that's what the incarnation means: it means God's truth and reality have become embodied within a particular human life, lived like, but unlike, all the others. When Jesus came to announce the coming of the kingdom of God, this was a truth embodied in his own person and life and it was to be embodied in the life of the communities of the kingdom that followed. The kingship of Jesus may from the outside sound just like another claim to mastery over others. However, this only points up the necessity, especially in this cultural setting, for an understanding of evangelism that makes it dependent on and tightly linked to the enactment of the loving rule of Christ within the Church's own life. If human life was always meant to be lived and to flourish under God's gentle and compassionate rule, then the Church, the community of the kingdom, has to embody that truth, to incarnate it, to use Christian language, if its proclamation is to be heard.

Notes

1 N. T. Wright, *Jesus and the Victory of God*, London, SPCK, 1996, pp. 275–97.
2 See, for example, Romans 10.9; 1 Corinthians 12.3.
3 Naturally St Paul did not use the language of the kingdom of God very often, yet he did clearly think in terms of the lordship of Christ, which we are arguing here is very close in meaning to the idea. For the essential harmony between Paul and Jesus on this theme, see David Wenham, *Paul: Follower of Jesus or Founder of Christianity?*, Grand Rapids, MI: Eerdmans, 1995, ch. 2.
4 Lesslie Newbigin, *The Gospel in a Pluralist Society*, London: SPCK, 1989, p. 227.
5 For example, see Galatians 1.8; Ephesians 2.17; 1 Thessalonians 3.6.
6 Newbigin, *Gospel*, p. 136.

CHAPTER 5

'Evangelism makes me
feel guilty'

---◆---

Fairly regularly I get to speak to church groups about evangelism. Often it's because they have decided they want to hold some kind of evangelistic programme, and they want to think a bit about what it will involve. I sometimes ask them how the word 'evangelism' makes them feel. I have found again and again that the word arouses one very common emotion in many Christians. It is not excitement, energy or prayerfulness. It is guilt.

Part of the problem is that most Christians agree that evangelism is a good thing. It's something Christians ought to do in some form or other. At the same time, however, most Christians also know that they don't do it, or if they do, they don't do it very well. The combination of knowing you ought to be doing something, and yet not actually having the courage, ability or time to do it, is a classic recipe for guilt.

In some churches this is compounded by the attitude of professional ministers and perhaps some influential lay people. The message coming from the front is that evangelism is the most important activity of the Church. In a sense they are right. What could be more important than getting people to believe in Christ, bringing those who don't know Christ to a real and enriching faith? As a result, every other sermon ends with a stirring appeal to 'get out there and tell your friends'. Some churches run endless evangelistic training courses, and those who are naturally gifted evangelists who go on or run these courses are made to feel the most valuable people in church. As we mentioned in the previous chapter, other church activities, such as worship, visiting the sick, running the church lunch club for local retired people, or preparing flowers to make the place look good on Sundays are seen as less important. Those whose gifts are in these areas, or perhaps those who are so bruised by life that they feel uncertain about being able to share their faith boldly with others, can begin to feel like second-class citizens.

It's unfortunate but true that under the surface, many Christians struggle with the idea of evangelism, and the more people talk about it, the worse they feel. As they are constantly reminded of evangelistic duties, which they find hard to fulfil yet others seem to manage quite easily, the result is a heavy heart and a quiet resolve not to listen the next time evangelism is mentioned. Sharing your faith is sometimes portrayed as the kind of thing that only those with a couple of theology degrees, an extrovert character and the emotional constitution of a rhinoceros would try. And because most of us aren't like that, we slink away, a little embarrassed, but greatly relieved.

So, how can we hold together all that the last few chapters have maintained about the centrality of evangelism to the Church's life and identity, along with the presence of other ministries and callings in the Church, and in particular, how can we ensure evangelism takes place without arousing the level of guilt that it often generates? And how can this understanding of evangelism as 'inviting people to come under the rule of God' help us here?

Provoking the question

Earlier on, we stressed the importance of creating desire and provoking questions. In the previous two chapters,

71

we saw the kingdom of God and the lordship of Christ as key themes, which lie at the heart of the theology of the Church. The two come together when we grasp that it is life under the kingdom of God that provokes the questions of the curious and even the uninterested.

A glance at the New Testament letter of 1 Peter can help develop this crucial point. In one of the best-known verses on evangelism in the whole of the New Testament, Christians are told: 'Always be prepared to give an answer to everyone who asks you to give the reason for the hope that you have. But do this with gentleness and respect' (1 Peter 3.15).

This verse regularly turns up in evangelism training courses. It seems to be a clear vindication of the attempt to get every Christian clued up with apologetic answers and gospel outlines, ready to explain to anyone within earshot. Yet the verse assumes something that isn't often noticed. It's really very simple, and really very important. *It assumes that someone has asked a question.* The scenario is presumably that a pagan neighbour has noticed something odd about this first-century Christian. Perhaps there is something vaguely different about them, summed up in the word 'hope'. Contemporary literature tells us that many Greco-Roman people were nervous about the inevitability of death and the fear of oblivion. Yet this Christian is somehow unconcerned; they even look forward to death as the gateway to something better. They have a level of expectation, a lack of fear about growing older and dying that the pagan cannot understand. So he asks the question, 'Why?' 'What is the reason for the hope that you have?' And that is the point at which the Christian is to proclaim their faith.

There is a world of difference between talking to someone who desperately wants to hear what you have to say, and someone who is listening out of politeness, or not listening at all. And Peter's first letter reminds us that creating desire is a crucial element of the evangelistic task.

The part of 1 Peter 3.15 that is usually left out (and was left out of the quotation above!) is the very first sentence, which comes before all the business about being prepared to give an answer. It is the simple phrase: *'In your hearts set apart Christ as Lord.'* It is also the most crucial part of the verse. As a Christian learns to live her life under the lordship of Jesus Christ, as she learns to adopt his perspective on money, sex, power, time and eternity and live her life in the light of these, then she will become the kind of person who provokes questions in the minds of her twenty-first-century non-Christian neighbours.

And it's not just for individuals. The verbs in this section of the letter are all plural. They are addressed to the Christian community, and so the instructions come to the Church as a whole rather than just individuals. Again here, the priority is to make every effort to 'live in harmony with one another; be sympathetic, love as brothers, be compassionate and humble. Do not repay evil with evil or insult with insult, but with blessing' (1 Peter 3.8–9).

This description lies very close to Jesus' description of the values which are to prevail in his communities of the kingdom. These are exactly the kind of things you find when God is really in charge and has his way; they are the things that proclaim that Jesus really has won the victory over sin and death and evil. A community that is marked strongly by deep and genuine sympathy, love, compassion and humility is hugely attractive. Again it provokes questions, leading to the occasion for explaining why it is like this. When the Church begins to be truly itself, it will not be able to stop itself being evangelistic.

The early chapters of Acts tell the story of one of the most significant evangelistic events in the history of the Church – Peter's sermon on the first day of Pentecost – where we are told that 3,000 people were added to the Church.

Again, it's fascinating to see the pattern at work here. The huge response was due not just to Peter being on good form that day with an incisive, articulate and rhetorically elegant sermon. Something very important happens before that. To their astonishment, the crowd, gathered in Jerusalem from the Jewish diaspora for the special sacrifices of the Feast of Weeks, hear the uneducated Galilean followers of Jesus speaking in their widely differing languages. They are so amazed and perplexed by this that they ask, '*What does this mean?*' (Acts 2.12). This is the vital question, and again, as we saw in 1 Peter, it becomes the occasion for the announcement of the gospel by Peter. The phenomenon needed explanation – on its own, this remarkable occurrence was just a puzzle – but it was the combination of an event that raised eyebrows and an interpretation that pointed to Jesus Christ as the reason for it that produced this remarkable result.

So, what is it that makes people 'ask the question'? The answer of 1 Peter is quite simple: 'Live such good lives among the pagans that, though they accuse you of doing wrong, they may see your good deeds and glorify God on the day he visits us' (1 Peter 2.12). The Greek word used here, *anastrophē*, generally means behaviour, or conduct; it is an all-encompassing word, and calls the Christians to a type of conduct that overcomes the negative preconceptions of Christianity. In the first century, accusations of immorality needed to be overcome; in the twenty-first it may be accusations of irrelevance. Either way, the idea is that those outside the Church need to see behaviour that is remarkable and unexpected.

The letter gives a number of different examples of the kind of thing it has in mind. The early Christians were often suspected of being socially subversive and refusing to recognize due authority; here, the Christians are told to submit to all legal authorities (1 Peter 2.13) – to do precisely the thing that was not expected. When a slave became a Christian, it might seem an affront to his master, implying that his gods were not good enough, inviting suspicion and abuse. Whether their masters are good or bad, Christian slaves are told to accept beatings, even (and perhaps especially) when they don't deserve it (2.18–20). When a wife became a Christian, this could often be seen as a declaration of independence from her husband, leading to marital strife. Christian wives are instead told to submit to their husbands, precisely so that they might be won over to Christ. Submission is recommended not because of gender inferiority, but evangelistic necessity – submission would be the last thing a pagan husband would expect from his religiously emancipated wife! In each case, behaviour is advised that is remarkable, unexplained and that provokes the question.

But are all these merely stunts to grab attention, arbitrary gestures to provoke a reaction? Some while ago, I heard of a student mission, where Christian students on campus hid in dustbins while their colleagues were about to come out of lectures. As they emerged from their classes, the Christian students would bang loudly on the dustbins, spring out like jack-in-the-boxes, and start preaching about their faith. An interesting gimmick perhaps, and it certainly took courage but, frankly, it sounds a bit odd. Is this what is being recommended – eye-catching and eccentric stunts to create interest?

The author of 1 Peter is much more subtle and theologically consistent than this. Each of these examples has a particular characteristic: they all possess a strong resonance with the behaviour (the *anastrophē*) of Jesus. Slaves are to accept unjust suffering. Why? 'Because Christ suffered for you, leaving you an example, that you should follow in his steps' (1 Peter 2.21). Christians are to be submissive to one another, to authorities and to marriage partners because Jesus was marked by submissiveness and mercy (3.17–18). All of the moral qualities and conduct recommended in the letter – whether humility, love, hospitality or generosity – are appropriate because they are Christ-like, and of course Jesus is the exact picture of what a human life looks like when lived under God's rule, in his kingdom.

There is a fascinating story from the early Church that illustrates the same point. Pachomius was an Egyptian who in the early years of the fourth century AD had been conscripted into the Roman army. He was taken down the Nile and was being held in a kind of cross between a prison and an army barracks near Luxor when he was visited by a strange group of local people with gifts of food and drink. Intrigued, he asked why they would come to visit someone they didn't know and had no obligation to. He received the answer that it was because they were followers of Jesus, and they had a custom of visiting those in prison as they would visit Jesus himself, just as their Lord had taught them. Pachomius was so impressed, he decided to become one of these 'Christians'. In time, he became one of the most important founders of communal Christian monasticism, the movement that served to keep Christianity alive during many of the dark days to come after the fall of the Roman Empire. Here is a prime example of Christ-like behaviour provoking a question, which is answered by the word of the gospel leading to a profound and active faith.

The place for the local church to start then is not with appeals to 'go and tell your friends'. In fact these vague, imprecise exhortations at the end of sermons often do more harm than good. They give little help as to how to do it, create unrealistic expectations, and so generate guilt. Instead, the Church is, in its own heart, to 'set apart Christ as Lord'. It is to seek to order its own life under the rule of God. This means governing its internal and external relationships, its structures and use of resources by the desire to live a Christ-like life – to live its life under the rule of God. This is not because evangelism is less important, but precisely because it is so important and primary, and because this is the way in which evangelism fits within the economy of the Church and the kingdom of God.

To the embarrassment of many an evangelist over the years, the epistles of the New Testament hardly ever contain appeals to Christians to get out and tell their friends about Jesus. And it's not because the New Testament writers were not concerned that people came to faith in Christ. It's just that they knew this was not the way it happens. The focus of these letters instead lies on getting these small Christian communities to order their lives under the rule of God, ensuring they are marked not with petty jealousies, arguments and competition, but instead by love, compassion and holiness. Hence the repeated insistence on the expression of Christian belief, not primarily in evangelistic activity, but in distinctive, provocative lives. (We'll look at this question more closely in Chapter 10.)

In one sense, talk about priorities for the Church is misleading, a wrong way to pose the question. If the Church exists to live and proclaim the kingdom of God and the lordship of Christ, then everything the Church does can have an evangelistic dimension. Caring for struggling marriages, visiting prisons, offering to mow the lawns of local elderly people, Sunday worship, prayer for healing, whatever the Church does is to be governed by the need to live under the rule of God, to live as if the decisive battle over sin and death has been won, and that Christ really is in charge. These things are valuable in their own right as demonstrations of what the world looks like when Jesus is acknowledged as king, even if they never result in any conversions. However, as they provoke questions they are to become the occasions for proclamation and explanation.

We've already touched on something of what this might mean for first-century Christians living in Asia Minor. To do the proper work of cultural transposition, we need to ask what this might mean for twenty-first-century Christians today. Illustration is one of the best teachers, so here are just a couple of examples from very different cultures to stimulate innovation and imagination.

Being neighbours

A pastor arriving in a church in a fairly run-down area of a large city realized that the church was making little impact on its neighbourhood. For many years, the church had just got older, and no one new had joined. As he talked to local people, he began to understand the kind of place it was. It was an urban area with lots of short-term accommodation and a high turnover of people. As few people stayed for long, no one bothered to get to know their neighbours and there was little sense of community in the area. People lived in isolation, and loneliness was a significant problem. He decided to get the church to learn together how to be good neighbours. They did Bible studies on the Good Samaritan, and what it taught about being a neighbour, and on Jesus' teaching about welcoming strangers in Matthew 25. Church members undertook to keep an eye out for people who moved into houses in the neighbourhood, and make sure they visited them to offer help within the first week. They found out dates of birthdays of children in local homes, and sent birthday cards on the right date. They kept a special eye out for elderly people, and when one of them fell ill, would mobilize the church to cook meals, drop in notes of concern and visit regularly.

The programme began to generate quite a bit of interest in the locality. As the Christians enacted the call to be good neighbours in simple, inexpensive but genuine ways, with no strings attached, a few people in the area began to ask why they were doing it. The answer came back, as they had learnt in their Bible studies, that it was because they were followers of Jesus, who had taught them to welcome strangers and visit those in need. A trickle began to turn up at church on Sundays and some signed up for an Alpha course. For the first time in years, the church began to grow.

Gutters and blood

A church in a small town in Malaysia was growing. The town was not a major centre, and social services were not as efficient as they might have been. In the heat of a tropical country, open gutters outside the church smelt badly, especially when garbage accumulated and the town council was slow to clear it. As church members arrived on Sunday, the smell would sometimes be overpowering. Repeated phone calls to the council got no response, so the church decided to clear the gutters themselves. Then someone pointed out that this was not just a problem for the church, it was a problem for the whole town. So, one Saturday, they got the whole church to turn out in dirty clothes armed with brushes and boots, and set to clearing as many of the town's gutters as they could. Townspeople were amazed that finally the drains were being cleared, but not by the town council. Naturally they asked who these people were and why they were doing it, which led to many intrigued people turning up at church over the next few weeks.

Having learnt something of the potential of this kind of thing, another need presented itself. The local hospital was having great difficulties collecting enough blood for surgical operations and transfusions. Many of the townspeople were of Chinese origin, and ancient Chinese beliefs about how giving blood would weaken and diminish them led to a marked reluctance to turn up to donate blood. The church decided it would promote a drive among its own members to do something about this. The hospital soon had a phone call from the church, and suddenly found a large increase in the number of people giving blood. Many doctors and nurses within the hospital as well as others in the town who came to hear of it were perplexed, interested and began to ask the church people why they were doing it. The blood donation programme was worth doing in its own right as a valid action expressing the love and sacrifice of Christ. It also provoked questions.

These are just examples. However, they illustrate some important insights. Both churches took a great interest in their local community and took the trouble to know it and its needs well. Both examples are closely adapted to their settings: to use theological jargon, they are both incarnational, expressing what God's rule means in a particular local setting. A programme of gutter-clearing would make little sense in an area where social services are efficient and regular, and being good neighbours would make little impact on a place that already has a strong sense of community.

Both were communal activities. If an isolated individual Christian had chosen to give blood or visit a neighbour, it would have had some impact, but not a great deal. That might just be explained by the fact that the person in question happened to be a bit more generous and kind than the average. It probably would not have raised too many eyebrows. Because a whole church did it, the impact was multiplied hugely. It became a community event, expressing something not just about an individual Christian, but about the Christian community itself. It's a much clearer statement that this is not just about nice people doing good deeds, but the kingdom of God made tangible.

The power of goodness

Even on the individual level, a life full of random or even planned acts of goodness and kindness is a provocative and startling thing. After you've made your order, when you come round to the payment kiosk at your local drive-thru McDonald's, why not occasionally pay the bill for the people in the car behind, asking the cashier just to tell them it was a gift? When you see a homeless person getting drenched in the rain, why not give him your umbrella? If you're asked for a pound (or a dollar) by the kid who comes to your door selling tea towels, why not give him five? The point about these actions is that they demonstrate the lavish goodness of God. They don't have to be accompanied by a little sermon or even a pre-printed card explaining that they are motivated by the love of God. They stand on their own as expressions of this rich, good and generous God who is the true king. St Augustine taught that all people everywhere are longing to find the true happiness that lies in the distant memory of the human race from our original intimacy

81

with God, lost since the fall. We search endlessly for this true happiness and goodness. Christians who give others a small taste of that goodness with such inexplicable acts of kindness can jog the memory, reawaken that desire for a God who is goodness itself.

Evangelism begins not with human actions, but God's action. Where his Spirit is at work, where his kingdom is active, there lives will be changed and questions will be raised. As Lesslie Newbigin says: 'It is impossible to stress too strongly that the beginning of mission is not an action of ours, but the presence of a new reality, the presence of the Spirit of God in power.'[1]

Guilty?

If evangelism makes you feel guilty, then it need not do. Anything done in the name of Christ and that points to his victory and kingship over the world has the potential of becoming an occasion for evangelism by raising the question. It doesn't mean that these actions of love or compassion are done with the *motive* of getting people interested. In line with the theological priority of bearing witness to the rule of God, these actions have an integrity of their own and can never simply be seen as a means to an end. Even if they never lead to anyone being converted, they are still worth doing and valuable in their own right. If they are to be expressions of the kingdom of God, then by definition, like the love of God, they need to be unconditional, with no strings attached. If they are genuine, however, they will provoke questions, and it is a false modesty as well as questionable theology to refuse to answer the question by pointing in some way to the one who inspires these very actions. If Jesus addressed his contemporaries both in signs and words, teaching and healing, then we too are to speak as well as

82

act. Christians don't worship a dumb God, so shouldn't be dumb themselves.

Naturally the big fear many Christians have at this point is how they can explain. Many of us worry that the words will not come, we will explain badly and inarticulately, and if difficult questions are raised, we won't know how to answer. That is when the gifts of the evangelist and the apologist come in. Courses for 'seekers', such as Alpha, are made for this moment. Often the best context in which to address difficult apologetic questions and convey basic Christian doctrine is in a long conversation that takes several weeks, in the context of worship, trust, care and honesty. It is precisely these things that something like Alpha provides. So the best option at this point may simply be to say something like: 'I'm probably not the best person to ask all these questions, but I do know a place where you can explore them and get some sensible answers.'

In the early Church, those who were genuinely intrigued by Christianity and its power to change individuals and communities were invited to join the catechumenate, a long process of instruction, discovery and investigation. It served a purpose because many ordinary Christians were often good at living out their faith but not so good at explaining it. A course like Alpha provides exactly the same service today. The problem many churches have is getting people to go on such courses in the first place. These churches might be better served encouraging the many Christians who don't feel very confident in evangelism to give time and energy to the kind of projects that express the reality of the rule of God in their local setting, alongside encouraging those who have gifts in evangelism and apologetics to use them in the setting of courses designed to include the exercise of such gifts.

Human life was always intended to be lived under the rule of God. Deep down it is what all of us long for, to live in a world where we love and are loved, where we treat each other and the whole created order with gentleness, humility and kindness, where we can be creative, hospitable, generous and forgiven. This is the place where we flourish best, even if we don't always recognize it. When we see a community of people living under God's rule in this way, it is immensely attractive. Communities where it is possible to taste and to learn love, joy, peace, patience, kindness, goodness, faithfulness, gentleness and self-control are rare but beautiful.

Earlier in this book, we touched on the heartfelt cry of Douglas Coupland's character to find somewhere he could learn generosity, kindness and love. Are not these the very characteristics of the kingdom of God? They're certainly not the values of many other kingdoms. There is an uncanny match between the deepest cries of human hearts in their best and clearest moments, and the values of God's kingdom, announced and inaugurated in Jesus. He is the master of generosity, kindness and love; he is the one who can teach and develop these things as we learn to live under his gentle rule, his disciplined protection. The disturbing question this leaves my local church with is this: if Coupland's character turned up next Sunday morning, would he learn these things there?

Note

1 Lesslie Newbigin, *The Gospel in a Pluralist Society*, London: SPCK, 1989, p. 119.

84

CHAPTER 6

Is my church worth going to?

It is Sunday evening. The service has got as far as the notices. The minister looks around and sees the same familiar faces that are there every Sunday evening. He gets up to remind everyone that next week there is a guest preacher, and they should really try to bring their friends to hear him. The congregation hardly blink, settle down for the sermon and are soon shuffling out of the doors at the end of another service. Next Sunday evening comes around. The guest preacher arrives, is given cups of tea and ushered into the church for the service to begin. As he walks in to take his seat at the front of the church, the minister looks around, and with a sinking feeling in his heart, sees the same familiar faces that are there every Sunday evening. No one has brought anyone new.

It's a scenario that's been played out in many churches, and has often led to them giving up on evangelism. For many decades, evangelism has depended on the specialist speaker, whether the big name in a tent or football ground, or the smaller scale 'guest service' in the local church. Some churches do see newcomers being brought in for special services, but for many, the strategy is more often than not frustrating. Despite encouragement, entreaty and even bribery, many church members seem reluctant to bring friends.

There are many plausible reasons for this. A post-modern culture is less likely to listen to authority figures pronouncing truth from six feet above contradiction. Many Christians are understandably wary of risking a good friendship by inviting someone to what might turn out to be a disastrous and embarrassing event. Yet underneath these obvious reasons, I suspect there is a deeper unease that often prevents Christians from bringing friends to church, and it is this: that in their heart of hearts, *they do not really want to be there themselves.*

If you go to church faithfully week in week out, yet if you're absolutely honest, it bores you rigid, you won't want a good friend to endure something which has even less relevance to their life than it does to yours. Unless church is connecting with the lives of those who are already committed Christians within a congregation, unless it is helping them mature as people and live better and more integrated lives, then all the notices in the world won't persuade them to bring friends to church. 'Come and be bored with me' is hardly the best line to attract people into church!

From his experience of building Saddleback church in California, Rick Warren makes the telling point: 'If most of our members never invite anyone to come to our church, what are they saying (by their actions) about the quality of what our church offers?'[1] Very often the reason why people are reluctant to bring friends to church is not the poor quality of what is on offer at 'guest services' on special Sundays, but the poor quality of what's on offer every Sunday. However, we're touching here on something much deeper than presentation, and it won't be solved by just a little tinkering with Sunday services. There is a more fundamental ideological issue, and it concerns our understanding of conversion. A church's view of conversion will often determine its approach to evangelism. This chapter therefore takes a good look at the meaning of conversion and how it influences the way we go about evangelism, and church members' willingness and ability to invite and assimilate newcomers.

Classic conversions

The classic model of conversion suggests an instantaneous change. The best-known and favourite conversions tend to follow the same pattern. Saul of Tarsus was confronted by Christ on the Damascus road, and was changed almost overnight from a rabid persecutor of the Christians to their keenest apologist. The great St Augustine heard a voice in a Milan garden, urging him to 'take up and read', upon which he picked up a copy of the letters of Paul, and experienced an instantaneous change of heart. In the popular version of the story, Martin Luther discovered his Reformation doctrine of justification by faith in a blinding flash of insight in a tower room of the Wittenberg Augustinian friary. John Wesley found his heart 'strangely warmed' while hearing Luther's commentary on Romans being read out at a meeting in London in 1738. All of them follow the classic pattern, and these stories, handed down from generation to generation, have tended to shape our understanding of conversion and led many a church to look for and recreate the crisis moment, in which an emotionally charged sinner is brought to release and sudden insight by the power of the Spirit.

In the New Testament also, we find language that suggests sudden and dramatic change. Imagery that depicts the difference between being a Christian and not being a Christian is very stark. It speaks of moving from death to life, from darkness into light, and being born again. You're either one or the other, not halfway between. Images of resurrection, birth and illumination all suggest a pretty instantaneous change.

The difficulty comes when we realize that many conversions are not experienced like this. In 1992, John Finney, who was at the time the Church of England's

Officer for the Decade of Evangelism, published some research that has become very influential, at least in British thinking on evangelism. His survey consulted around 500 people who had recently made public professions of Christian faith, and perhaps its most significant finding was that 69 per cent of those asked described their conversion as 'gradual' rather than 'sudden'.[2] In fact this still leaves 31 per cent (quite a sizeable proportion!) who did think of their conversion as datable to a day or moment but, nonetheless, this seems good evidence that the classic sudden conversion is far from the norm.

Alongside other indications, this evidence has led to a much greater adaptation of evangelistic methods to the supposedly gradual nature of conversion. In a survey of changing attitudes to evangelism in the 1990s, Robert Warren notes:

> It can be said that the 'evangelistic appeal' has changed from 'I want you to get up out of your seats and come forward now . . .' to 'we invite you to join a group that will be exploring the Christian faith over the coming weeks at . . .'. Behind this shift in practice is a shift in perception, namely that faith is a journey and takes time. Coming to faith itself, not just the work of evangelism, is now seen as a process.[3]

There are of course good cultural reasons to explain why conversions may happen more gradually nowadays. In John Wesley's day, there was a much more general knowledge of basic Christian beliefs. God's existence was assumed, and it was merely a matter of making this dead faith live. It was as if the understanding of Christian belief was lying there like a large bonfire of dry wood – it just needed a spark of fire to set it off.

Now, the bonfire needs first to be built, long before the spark can light the fire. As many people know less of what Christian faith claims, it takes longer to build basic understanding of what being a real Christian involves than it used to. But does this therefore mean that the classic dramatic conversion is a fake, an attractive, but ultimately empty illusion?

Process or crisis?

Lewis Rambo, author of an important multidisciplined study of the subject, suggests that the way conversion takes place is shaped by both the expectations of those urging the necessity of conversion, and the past experiences of the one being converted. He sees it as a process, which may also include some crisis moments: 'While it can be triggered by particular events, and in some cases, result in very sudden experiences of change, for the most part, it takes place over a period of time.'[4]

Rambo's perspective on this makes a lot of sense. When we look more closely at the four classic conversions above, each crisis moment can be seen in the context of a much longer process. Before he became Paul the apostle, the book of Acts tells us that Saul of Tarsus witnessed the impressive and moving martyrdom of Stephen, and in his own writings, he sees his earlier training in Pharisaic Judaism as a kind of preparation for the gospel. As his *Confessions* shows, Augustine's experience in Milan came at the climax of a long period of intellectual and spiritual searching, during which he had listened intently to the teaching of Bishop Ambrose of Milan, read Christian texts and engaged in long discussions with Christian friends.[5] Most Luther scholars now see his Reformation discovery as taking place gradually over a period of a number of years, rather than being confined to one blinding flash of light.[6] Long before his 'Aldersgate experience', even John Wesley was searching for illumination during his time as an unsuccessful missionary to Georgia and as a priest in the Church of England. Crises usually come in the middle or at the end of processes.

How then do we reconcile biblical imagery indicating the stark difference between being a Christian and not being a Christian with the gradual way in which the transition is often experienced? In this discussion, it is important to distinguish theological from phenomenological perspectives. On the one hand, *theologically* it is possible and even important to hold firmly to the biblical notion of the distinctness of spiritual life in Christ and death without him, òr to use theological jargon again, being regenerate or unregenerate. Yet at the same time *phenomenologically* we can recognize that the events surrounding this transfer are often experienced as a process, and the moment of transfer is not often registered. It's also possible to hold alongside this the idea that the experienced phenomenon of conversion is subject to a wide range of social, psychological, cultural and religious factors that can legitimately be analysed by social scientists. The Christian, however, will want to insist that these factors don't entirely explain conversion, as they cannot capture the divine and spiritual dimensions of the event.

Regeneration and transformation

In thinking about conversion, it may help to explain the difference between *regeneration* and *transformation*. 'Regeneration' is a theological word that talks about the stark change from spiritual death to life, from being outside of Christ or in him, being forgiven or unforgiven. 'Transformation' on the other hand is a process that may begin long before and continue after a person consciously 'becomes a Christian', in which a person is gradually changed from an unbeliever in Christ to someone who increasingly bears the image of Christ, living their life under God's rule. Conversion can be thought of as encompassing both of these – the momentary transfer, as the letter to the Colossians puts it, from the 'dominion of darkness' to the 'kingdom of the Son', *and* the lifelong process of change.

It's important both to distinguish these things, yet also to hold them together. If we have no concept of sudden regeneration, we can end up thinking that there is no real difference between being a Christian and not being a Christian. We may have little sense of the radical difference God can make to human lives when they open themselves to his life-giving Spirit, and a diminished sense of assurance that we are Christ's once and for all. If we have no concept of gradual transformation, we will end up leaving new Christians high and dry, and quickly bored with their new-found faith. We will also fail to obey the simple command of the New Testament, to 'become mature, attaining to the whole measure of the fulness of Christ' (Ephesians 4.13).

A helpful image at this point is the one coined by John's Gospel, when it speaks of 'seeing the kingdom of God' as like being born a second time (John 3.3). When my wife was expecting our first child, I remember everything being focused on the labour and the birth itself. How would she get through it? Would the baby be OK? Would I faint during the birth? It seemed such a huge event to get past. Pregnancy had already made dramatic differences to our lives as my wife struggled through a hot summer feeling heavier and heavier, needing to rest more and more. When our son finally arrived, although it shouldn't have been a surprise, it dawned on me that this was not the end of the process, it was the beginning! New life had come into the world and now needed feeding, nurturing and enjoying. Birth is a crisis that comes after a process of preparation, and is a stage (though quite an important one!) in a much longer process of growth and new life beyond it.

As Robert Warren suggests and Lewis Rambo confirms, our understanding of conversion will shape our practice of evangelism. The more we conceive of conversion as a process, the more we will put our energies into 'process evangelism' strategies, such as courses for seekers. The more we see it as a crisis, the more eggs we will put in the basket of one-off events, whether evangelistic sermons or tent crusades. Any approach to evangelism today that wants to be faithful to Scripture and sensitive to culture will want to ensure elements of both of these. Too much 'process' and the distinctiveness and assurance of being a Christian may be lost. Too much 'crisis' and we may end up forcing people into a mould that they don't fit. 'Process' courses in evangelism also need to make space for crisis moments. Transformation needs to make space for regeneration in the course of conversion.

Preaching to the converted?

Our understanding of conversion doesn't just affect the way we go about our evangelism, however. It also has a big impact on our motivation for it in the first place. A number of years ago, a very wise and perceptive South African Christian friend wrote to me about a number of personal difficulties he had been struggling with. He described these anxieties in a fascinating way: 'These things have reminded me of how much there remains in me that needs to be converted.' His words lingered on in my mind long after I had replied to and thrown away the letter. Here was a man fully committed to Christ, a converted man if ever there was one, yet here he was saying that the process of conversion had not yet finished.

We sometimes tend to think of Christians, fully paid-up members of our churches, as 'the converted', and those who are not yet Christians as the ones who need converting. This can then lead to neglect of the Christians in preference for those who still need to be 'converted', namely the non-Christians. After all, doesn't the shepherd leave the 99 sheep slumbering in the fold while he goes out after the one lost one?

Unfortunately this is a disastrous strategy, whether you're a shepherd or a church leader. A shepherd who has no interest in making sure his entire flock finds good pasture, and remains healthy and strong, will quickly find he has a lot fewer than 99 sheep left, as they either die off under the rigours of winter, or sneak away to find better shepherds. Leaders too will find much the same happening in their churches.

If they are to be effective evangelistically, churches need to be interested not just in regeneration but also in transformation. Not just in getting people to become Christians, but in having a clear agenda of spiritual and personal growth beyond the moment or process of becoming a Christian. Or to put it another way, conversion has to be seen as not just a momentary event, but also a lifelong reality. This is important not just so that Christians can move on and grow, not just for the sake of effective pastoral care, but for the sake of evangelism itself.

Evangelism leads to transformation

When I was training for church leadership, I was sent for practical experience on weekly visits to a home for severely mentally and physically disabled adults. I and a couple of other eager, well-meaning theological students decided to run a series of short services where we tried to explain the gospel as simply as we could, with visual aids and the rest. It didn't take long to realize that we weren't connecting well. One of the residents would look out of the window the whole time, a couple would talk to each other, another would drum his fingers on the chair loudly and repeatedly, and another would get up and walk around the room when she felt like it.

It was pretty clear that the ideas we were explaining about God and Jesus were not having the desired effect. Through conversations I was beginning to get to know some of them well, enjoying their company and their special character, but they did not seem to be able to respond to a 'normal' presentation of the gospel, however simple, in the way I had come to expect – by a clear decision to follow Christ, expressed in words, after having considered what this call to discipleship meant.

As the weeks went by, the evangelist in me began wondering what an appropriate response to the gospel would be for them. What did I expect them to do, and how could I tell if they had responded? Were they unable to respond to God's grace and love? Surely that conclusion was out of the question. They may have been different from other people, but if they still bore the image of God, that must mean they were capable of a response to him. Yet that response was not going to be primarily verbal, rational, intellectual or articulate. Rightly or wrongly, I came to the conclusion that their response to God was their response to whatever love or mercy they experienced in the name of Christ, probably expressed more in their own actions, choices and behaviour than in words.

Yet this wasn't the end of it. As I came to think that it was possible for a person to respond to God in other ways than the primarily rational and cerebral, I began to think about others who perhaps responded to God in these ways. What about those who don't or can't read books? What about those who don't tend to think things through logically (do any of us)? Perhaps the rational consent of the mind that I had been looking for was not the heart of the matter? Sure, it was important for those with the ability to use their minds in this way, but maybe responding to God was not just a matter of getting my thinking straight?

These experiences opened my eyes to the possibility that responding to God was not only or primarily a rational and intellectual thing. There was a lot more of me that remained to be converted, as well as those to whom I was speaking. Conversion meant bringing the whole of my life (not just my mind) under the rule of God.

Jesus was once asked the question many of us would probably want to ask him: 'What is the meaning of life?' In the language of the day, the question went: 'What is the greatest commandment?', but this is pretty much what it meant. His reply was remarkable. Picking up the language of Deuteronomy, his answer to that million-dollar question is that human life is about learning to 'love the Lord your God with all your heart and with all your soul and with all your mind and with all your strength'. The next most important thing was learning to love your neighbour as if he were yourself (Mark 12.28–31). It's hard to know precisely what the difference is between heart, soul, mind and strength, but taken together, it speaks of learning to love God with every part of our lives, emotions, will and intellect; with our bodies, minds and spirits. It means a reorientation of our lives towards learning to love God and learning to love other people, rather than the self-indulgent and self-oriented lives we're used to. Paul has a similar idea in Ephesians, where he prays that God will:

> strengthen you with power through his Spirit in your inner being, so that Christ may dwell in your hearts through faith. And I pray that you, being rooted and established in love, may have power, together with all the saints, to grasp how wide and long and high and deep is the love of Christ, and to know this love that surpasses knowledge – that you may be filled to the measure of all the fulness of God. (Ephesians 3.16–19)

Paul writes here of Christ dwelling not just in the mind, but also in the 'inner being'. The love of Christ is something that 'surpasses knowledge' – it cannot be grasped fully by the mind, but needs to be 'grasped' in a much fuller way by the whole person. And the goal that covers the whole exercise is being filled with 'all the fulness of God'. This is a breathtaking and expansive vision of what conversion means. It is the transformation from a life lived in purely human terms, to one where every part of a person's existence is gradually brought under God's rule. It involves the transformation of heart, soul, mind and strength. It involves the invasion of the Holy Spirit to the depths of a person's very being. It involves a comprehensive grasp of how deeply we are loved, which goes far beyond the mere intellectual acknowledgement of the fact. It is about a life soaked in love for God and love for those we meet each day. It is about responding to God with all that we have and all that we are, the way that we were always intended to.

In this sense, conversion never ends. Regeneration happens once as we are brought to a new life in Christ. Yet like natural birth, it takes its place as part of a larger process, God's destiny for human life.

The problem is that in many churches, little attention is paid to this ongoing process of transformation. It's not hard to find churches that are good at getting people to become Christians. Alpha courses, seeker services and the like are all excellent approaches to this task. It's more difficult to think of successful courses for those who have already been Christians for 20 years. These people are usually the ones whose rank is displayed by their places on church committees, and in holding official church positions. Yet so often that seems the only mark of growth in Christian life; it's easy to mistake church seniority for spiritual maturity.

These long-term Christians can easily stagnate and fossilize spiritually. Most people drift out of church not because they stop believing – they drift out because it ceases to be relevant to their lives. Robin Gill, a British theologian and sociologist, points out that 'most people change churchgoing habits when something else is changing in their lives'.[7] Reaching adolescence, getting married, having babies, moving house, losing a job – all these things lead us to re-evaluate our lives. But the point is not just that these things can lead to someone starting going to church; they can also lead to a person stopping going to church as well. If during this process of re-evaluation I reach the conclusion that church no longer has anything meaningful to say to these new issues I face, then it's quite possible that I may give up going altogether. Many people who leave church do so not because they have given up on faith or out of lack of attention to the Spirit. They leave because they no longer find anything spiritually satisfying or enriching there. They continue the journey of faith, but do it elsewhere.[8]

In Georges Bernanos' classic French novel, *The Diary of a Country Priest*, the young *curé* is scornful of the idea of losing faith: 'Faith is not a thing which one "loses", we merely cease to shape our lives by it.'[9] He's right of course. Rarely does a person lose faith because she decides it is no longer true; it is more often because it no longer seems relevant. And then it slowly gets put to the back of her life and factors other than God's kingdom begin to call the shots.

If this is to be arrested, it is vital that churches take this issue of transformation seriously. They have to keep in mind the goal of the transformation of individuals and communities, in the real practical details of life, so that people learn how to live well and Christianly in their family, work and friendships, not just in church. When churches evangelize, they need to keep in mind the long-term goal of producing transformed people, lifelong apprentices of Jesus Christ in the art of living well. Evangelism must lead to transformation.

Transformation leads to evangelism

The remarkable thing is that when the spiritual and personal growth of Christians is high on the agenda of a church, it also begins to be more effective evangelistically.

I remember some years ago being involved in a church where the members seemed strangely demotivated for evangelism, despite the fact that this was the church's number one stated goal, of which they were constantly reminded in almost every sermon. After a while, I began to work out why this was. Now that they were Christians, they were taught that their main job was to win others for Christ. Pastoral care was available if they really had serious problems, but the assumption was that they wouldn't need it, if they were walking with Christ. The leadership of the church were well-intentioned, eager people, who thought they were being fully evangelistic by this strategy of talking about little else. The result was exactly the opposite. Again and again I met people who felt their real needs were not being addressed – they were not getting help in Christian ways of bringing up their children, doing their jobs or spending their money. Personal struggles could not be admitted, needs for growth were ignored. It was a community full of unrealistic expectations, unmet needs and competing agendas. These are the classic symptoms of an unhappy marriage. They're also the classic symptoms of an unhappy church.

Churches where members are not experiencing this gradual transformation, leading them to live more mature, integrated, authentic lives, do not evangelize, however much they are told to from the front. It's worth repeating: if church members don't find much in church that speaks to their lives Monday through Saturday, then it's unlikely they'll want to bring others to be part of it.

However, in churches where people experience this expectation of transformation, where the worship is energizing, the teaching wise and insightful, the sense of community genuine, it's difficult to stop them bringing friends. Because deep down we long to learn generosity, kindness and love, to find those things is a precious thing. And if you find a place that can teach them to you, then you want your friends to have a piece of it too. In order to be fully human, we need, as Jesus himself put it, to learn to be poor in spirit, meek, hungry for justice, merciful, pure, peaceful and to suffer for other people's sake. The place to learn these things is in the kingdom of God. And when the Church begins to be like that kingdom, it begins to be immensely attractive. In other words, where Christians can experience what it means to have their lives increasingly brought under God's rule in Christ, then they will naturally want others to find the same reality for themselves. A transforming church is an evangelistic church.

For this reason, it's probably better to put the question of church health before church growth. Healthy things grow, and unhealthy things don't (or if they do, they grow in deformed ways). A little while ago, some friends had a litter of kittens. Most seemed fit and well-formed, and with only a little feeding and care from their mother, they soon grew bright-eyed and alert. One, however, looked weak and sickly. From the start, this one was clearly unhealthy. It had difficulty taking in food, and while the others grew firm muscle and sleek fur, this one remained a bag of bones. It was no great surprise when it eventually died. The key to growth is health. Healthy things grow – this is one of the basic rules of life in God's world. And the Church is not exempt from this rule.

Techniques of church growth are sometimes useful and effective but they will work only where there is a basic level of health in a church's inner life, its relationships and ministry. They can sometimes force growth in unhealthy churches by masking the problems, but the rule still applies – growth in unhealthy organisms is often deformed and unpleasant and leads in the long run to greater pain and discomfort.

This is not a recommendation for perfect churches. I've never yet seen one of these, and don't expect ever to do so this side of the age to come. There is no such thing as a 'successful church', if by that we mean a church that perfectly reflects the kingdom of God. Churches are hospitals for the sick, not gatherings of the strong. Church is always full of broken, imperfect people. The difference between an unhealthy and a healthy church, however, is whether these people are slowly being put together again by God's Holy Spirit, or whether being part of church is frankly making them worse. Where people are being made whole again, and are learning these vital life skills of love, generosity, suffering and kindness, as they learn of this kind God who loves, gives and suffers, then other people are drawn towards it. Transformation leads to evangelism.

Growing churches?

In church, are we preaching to the converted? Perhaps the minister looking out at his congregation at the start of this chapter thought he was. Perhaps he felt that now these people were Christians all he had to do was encourage them to bring their friends. Yet as we've seen, in an important sense, conversion never ends, and to treat a congregation as if they have no more need for personal change or maturity is to ensure that they will never engage wholeheartedly with evangelism. To put it slightly differently, to separate out evangelism from spiritual growth and maturity is a fatal mistake. The two are inextricably linked, and depend on each other.

This means that if a church wants to be effective evangelistically, it had better not start with evangelism. This is by no means to relegate evangelism to the back-burner. It is, however, to locate it properly within a church's own self-understanding. Instead, the church had better start with just trying to be itself. What that means we'll explore in the next chapter.

Notes

1 Rick Warren, *The Purpose Driven Church: Growth without Compromising Your Message and Mission*, Grand Rapids, MI: Zondervan, 1995, p. 52.
2 John Finney, *Finding Faith Today: How Does it Happen?* Swindon: BFBS, 1992, p. 24.
3 Robert Warren, *Signs of Life: How Goes the Decade of Evangelism?* London: Church House Publishing, 1996, p. 65.
4 Lewis R. Rambo, *Understanding Religious Conversion*, New Haven, CT: Yale, 1993, p. 165.
5 See St Augustine, *Confessions*, translated by Henry Chadwick, Oxford: OUP, 1992, Book VIII, pp. 133–54.
6 See for example W. D. J. Cargill Thompson, 'The Problem of Luther's "Tower Experience" and its Place in his Intellectual Development' in *Studies in the Reformation: Luther to Hooker*, ed. C. W. Dugmore, London: Athlone Press, 1980, pp. 60–80; Alister E. McGrath, *Luther's Theology of the Cross: Martin Luther's Theological Breakthrough*, Oxford: Basil Blackwell, 1985, p. 176; H. A. Oberman, *The Dawn of the Reformation: Essays in Late Medieval and Early Reformation Thought*, Edinburgh: T&T Clark, 1986, p. 40.
7 Robin Gill, *A Vision for Growth: Why your Church Doesn't Have to be a Pelican in the Wilderness*, London: SPCK, 1994, p. 65.
8 Alan Jamieson, *A Churchless Faith*, London: SPCK, 2002.
9 Georges Bernanos, *The Diary of a Country Priest*, translated by Pamela Morris, Glasgow: Collins, 1937, p. 105.

CHAPTER 7

Transforming communities

———◄●►———

A few years ago a friend of mine walked into his local church, expecting a normal midweek Bible study. As he entered, he saw a group of people sitting around in a circle as usual, so took a seat, noticing absent-mindedly that there seemed quite a few new people this week. In fact, as he looked closer, he realized that he didn't recognize anyone in the group at all. Looking at his watch, it dawned on him that he had got the wrong day, and had stumbled into the wrong meeting. By this stage, however, it had started, so he could hardly leave. A middle-aged woman was speaking about the kind of week she'd had, and how she had managed to avoid 'it' (whatever 'it' was) for most of the week apart from a few minor slips. As each person took their turn to speak, my friend realized he had stumbled into a meeting of the local branch of Alcoholics Anonymous.

Before long he mumbled some embarrassed apologies and left, but not before the meeting had made quite an impression on him. There seemed a measure of honesty, admission of failure, celebration of success and mutual encouragement in a common struggle that he had rarely found in the previous weekly Bible study meetings, which had often been rather dry academic discussions by comparison. The people who had gathered for the alcoholics' meeting came because they knew they needed help. They were anything but a respectable gathering of well-brought-up citizens doing the socially acceptable thing. They were desperate and wanted to change. And the group was slowly helping them do just that. He found himself wishing that church was a little more like this. He had accidentally discovered something about church that his own experience of it had not taught him: that it was intended to be a transforming community.

In the previous chapter, we looked at how evangelism needs to lead to the transformation of individuals and communities, and how conversely, transformation generates evangelism. But what does transformation actually mean? The kind of transformation offered by Alcoholics Anonymous is freedom from addiction to alcohol, but what kind does the Church offer? Moreover, how does it happen? How can we help grow churches that can transform both individuals and communities, and generate effective evangelism?

Life under the rule of God

As we have seen, the Church is to model its life on the kingdom, even though this side of the resurrection, it will always fall short. Yet the kingdom of God can seem an abstract idea – where are the models for what it looks like?

D. L. Moody once said that 'the world is yet to see what God can do with a man wholly given over to him'. Again it's one of these statements that carries a germ of truth, but only a half-truth. The world *has* already seen what God can do with a man living wholly under his rule, in the person of Jesus. So if we ask what a transformed person looks like, someone who lives their life under God's rule, well, they will look very much like Jesus. Of course adjustments need to be made for culture, time and language, but in essence, the unlimited forgiveness, unconditional love and brave opposition to all that is evil that Jesus displayed will be present in the life of any individual or group who seeks to live under God's rule today.

It's worth exploring this point a little more closely, to see exactly what this claim means. It involves delving into a branch of theology known as 'Christology' or, in other words, how we understand the person of Jesus Christ. In the earliest centuries of the Church, its best thinkers pondered this long and hard. Their debates can seem complicated and obscure at times, but the issues they grappled with were vital to understand. Whether we know it or not, how we understand Jesus has a big impact on our approach to just about everything in the Christian life, including evangelism itself.

Jesus – the divine human

At the beginning of the fourth century, the Church emerged from the shadows of persecution and suspicion to be adopted by the new Roman emperor Constantine as his own chosen faith. The Church was invited to begin shaping the Roman Empire from the centre. Yet if it was to do this, it was vital that it worked out exactly what it believed. Jesus was Lord, God's king – that declaration had been central to Christian theology from the earliest days – but how exactly was he connected to God? Was he a particularly excellent example of a man? Was he partly divine, like some of the figures in Greek mythology, or even the apotheosized emperors of recent times? Or was he fully divine? And if he was, how could he also be fully human? These were vital questions which touched on the Church's very identity, and as a result were hotly debated.

Around this time, a slender and serious-minded priest from Alexandria called Arius began teaching that Jesus was the Son of God only in the sense that he was closer

105

to God than any other human being. To preserve the central biblical insight of the uniqueness of God, he believed that Jesus the Son should be seen as the highest pinnacle of creation, but only that – a part of the created order, not part of God. God was unique and indivisible; if Jesus was in some way divine, that would mean dividing God in two. So, he reasoned, Jesus could not be said to share the same nature as God. After a longish debate, the Council of Nicaea in AD 325 took the opposite view, coining a new Greek word, *homoousios*, which indicated that Jesus was 'of one being' with the Father (we still say it in the Nicene Creed today) – he shared God's very nature.

Nicaea by no means finished off the debate, however. In the following years, as Arius' views remained popular, it was left to another Alexandrian, the abrasive and fiery Athanasius, to defend the Nicene position. Athanasius felt that Arius' view threatened the whole possibility of salvation. We humans had originally been created to be a mirror of God's goodness. We bore the imprint or image of God's very nature and shared his ability to love, be generous and wise, and to live for ever. Our true identity lay in our likeness to God, and to be fully human meant to share God's nature of love. Through Adam's act of primeval disobedience, however, we had forfeited that likeness to God, and instead had become subject to physical decay and folly. In other words, we became less than fully human, consumed by desire, not for God and all that is good, but for the very things that destroy life: selfish pleasure and prideful hostility. 'Adulteries and thefts were everywhere, murder and rape filled the earth, law was disregarded in corruption and injustice, all kinds of iniquities were perpetrated by all, both individually and corporately.'[1]

Athanasius' description of the human condition is not far off the mark. Jacques Ellul and even Terry Eagleton, whom we met earlier on, would agree. His point, however, is that this behaviour is evidence of a deeper malaise: that we have lost our dignity as god-like people. Compared to the staggering greatness of what we were intended to be, we have become faint shadows of our true selves. We have become more like animals than gods. We have become diminished, dehumanized and destined for death. In losing the divine image, we have lost our true humanity.

God's dilemma then was how to restore that divine likeness. Athanasius pictures God as presented with a momentous choice – to abandon his spoiled creation as no longer worthy of his love, or in that very love, to act to transform the human situation. God chooses the latter course, despite the cost to himself. For Athanasius, the solution to this dilemma was the incarnation, the coming of God into human flesh, to restore the divine image to humanity:

> What then was God to do? What else could he do but renew his Image in mankind, so that through it, men might once more come to know Him? And how could this be done, save by the coming of the very Image himself, our saviour Jesus Christ?[2]

Simply calling on us to try a little harder, to be sorry and see if we can do better next time, would fail to address the root of the problem. What is needed is a change of inner nature, not external performance. Disobedience is a rampant disease, which threatens to destroy us unless a radical antidote is found. The problem is not just a few minor moral slip-ups, but the tragic loss of the divine image. If this is true, argues Athanasius, the only way in which this can be restored is if the divine image is restored into humanity. Only God himself can do this, so it is essential for Athanasius that Jesus is not just the best of creation (as Arius had taught), a good example of how good a human life can get, but that he shares the divine nature, restoring it to humanity, so that we can share it too. If Jesus were only human, then he could no more restore the divine image than you or I could, however good a human he was. Christ then voluntarily submits to death, to pay the debt owed by humanity to death, and by his resurrection, he reverses the inevitable path to corruption and decay. Now, it's as if a sick humanity has had a renewed injection of life – the divine image has entered again to restore us, to reverse the inevitable outcome of the illness and restore us to full health, to our true selves.

Athanasius uses an illustration to make his point. He imagines an artist having painted a portrait, which has then become defaced through damage and abuse. Rather than throw away the valuable canvas, the artist patiently redraws the image, so that it is restored to its pristine state. Once the image of God in humanity has been defaced by sin and disobedience, rather than dispensing with the whole thing, God the divine artist redraws the image of God in human form – a picture of what human-ity was meant to be like – and he does this in the person of Jesus. Jesus is both a picture of the perfect human life and, at the same time, the perfect image of God. To be perfectly like God is to be perfectly human.

After Athanasius' time, the debate continued down a different track. Having asserted that Jesus shared God's very nature, the question became a matter of how Jesus' divine nature was related to his humanity. Just as the first question had reached something of a resolution at the Council of Nicaea in 325, the second question reached a conclusion of sorts at the Council of Chalcedon in 451. Here, the Council distanced itself from some ideas associated with the controversial Bishop of Constantinople, Nestorius, which implied that Jesus' humanity and divinity were two entirely different things, kept in separate compartments, as if they were entirely alien substances coexisting in the same body. While not falling into the opposite mistake of entirely obliterating the distinction between Christ's human and divine nature, the Council insisted that he was 'the same perfect in divinity, the same perfect in humanity, truly God and truly man'. In other words, Jesus the Son of God was a perfect picture of God. He was at the same time a perfect picture of a human being. The point the Chalcedonian fathers were trying to make was essentially the same as the one Athanasius was insisting on in a different context: that to be perfectly like God is to be perfectly human, and we have a real-life picture of what that means in Jesus himself.

The point of this venture into the realms of ancient Christology is simple: the more like God we become, the more human we become, not less. For Athanasius, salvation means becoming like God, having the divine image restored within us. At the same time, it means becoming more fully human, being restored to what we were originally meant to be. The fathers of Chalcedon were saying the same thing in a different context: Jesus is both the perfect image of God, and the perfect image of what a man should look like. And this is no accident. It's not that Jesus is fully human *despite* the fact that he was fully divine; it's precisely *because* Jesus is fully divine that he is so perfectly human. It's not as if humanity and divinity are two quite different things like stone and water, which have precious little in common. They are distinct, but because we were created to bear God's likeness or image, it is possible, even necessary for humanity to 'participate in the divine nature' (2 Peter 1.4).

A moment's thought shows how this makes sense. When you think of the qualities that characterize the God of the Bible, you probably think of his love, mercy, forgiveness, creativity, faithfulness, generosity and so on. When you think of the best people you know, those who seem most fully human, examples of humanity at its best, you probably end up thinking of the same kind of things – these are people full of love, mercy, forgiveness, creativity, faithfulness and generosity. Again, the more like God you become, the more fully human you are.

Talk of 'perfection' can make us think of abstract ideals in stained-glass windows, far removed from friendships, hospitality, work and sport, the stuff out of which real life is made. Yet when we call Jesus 'perfect man', we are to think not so much of ethereal and untouchable faultlessness, but rather of the best kind of person we can ever imagine – someone whose friendships were always deep, whose hospitality was forever welcoming, whose work was thorough, and whose play was rich and full of laughter.

Even still, asserting that Jesus is divine can seem to distance him from us, and many theologies in the past have reinforced that, ending up with a Jesus so remote and frightening that we have to bring in all kinds of other mediators, such as his mother or various past saints, to enable us to relate to him at all. Yet if we take seriously what the early Christians were saying, we can see that in a very important sense, recognizing Jesus as possessing and reflecting the image of God brings him nearer to us, not further away from us; it makes him more relevant, not less. He becomes not a distant, unattainable phantom, but an image of what we are called to be, and one day, in the grace of God, we can be.

Sometimes, we worry that if we really took Christianity seriously we would become weird and eccentric. And there are enough examples around of strange religious people who reinforce that fear. An intense interest in religion or church for its own sake can become as unbalanced as any other human activity, and is in itself no guarantee of this transformation. An intense interest in the true God, however, is a very different thing. Athanasius reminds us that to come closer to God is to fulfil our true humanity, that to submit to Jesus as Lord is in fact the most liberating thing we can do. It is not to become abnormal and odd, it is in fact to become the most normal people there are.

Becoming human again

So, the Church is to be an arena in which people can be transformed into full humanity, the image of God, which means to live like Jesus, fully under the rule of God. Evangelism must therefore bear this constantly in mind. It is not about filling the waiting room for heaven with a few more customers; it is inviting people to the transformed life of the kingdom, lived as fully and as daringly as possible here, and then fulfilled and perfected in the age to come. It is the invitation to become part of a community in which, individually and together, people are being transformed to being more like Jesus. It means becoming more generous, humble, joyful and alive, and less marked by those features that diminish us as people, whether arrogance, jealousy, bitterness or cruelty.

This means that the Church today is to be like Jesus. Not just individual Christians – yes they too are called to be like him in their own way – but the Church as a whole was always intended to remind people of Jesus. It is meant to recall the world to her proper destiny, to remind her of her true king, and to show her a picture of human life as it was originally intended to be.

This is where the rest of Christian theology comes in. In one sense, trying to be like Jesus is a contradiction in terms. Trying to restore the divine image within us is as fruitful as trying to play tennis like a Wimbledon champion when you're no good at the game. The only way in which this can begin to happen is if a much deeper change takes place.

A heroin addict needs first to be cleaned up from the physical effects of his addiction. He then needs to start the path of transformation from a way of life centred around drugs to something very different. Alcoholics Anonymous know all about this: 'We who are in AA came because we finally gave up trying to control our drinking.' The famous 12 steps of AA begin with a recognition of the problem, move on to the conviction 'that a Power greater than ourselves could restore us to sanity', and end with a wholly different pattern of behaviour.

Christian theology pulls no punches. It also thinks of us all, bluntly, as addicts. We may not be addicted to drugs or drink, but we remain addicted to a life centred on ourselves rather than God, to putting our own interests before those of others – these are the unmistakable signs of our loss of god-likeness. Like the alcoholic unable to resist the lure of a quick whisky on the side, we find ourselves similarly unable to resist for long the sly comment that puts down a colleague at work, or the indolence that watches the sufferings of others and does nothing about them. Our ability to love with all our hearts is about as effective as an alcoholic's self-control.

Transformation similarly begins with realizing that we were created clean, but have become soiled. It continues with being cleansed – this is what the atonement is about: Christ dying for our sins, so that they can be forgiven and we might begin again with a clean slate. In one sense this is the crucial part – on the basis of simply trusting this promise of forgiveness, we can know we are forgiven, acceptable before God. However, God has not finished with us there. His work in us continues with this restoration of the divine image; this god-likeness (or godliness, if you prefer), which is the work not of human effort but the Holy Spirit, God himself transforming us from within, replacing selfish desires with generous ones, destructive habits with creative ones. If Alcoholics Anonymous members always remain 'recovering alcoholics', Christians are always 'recovering sinners'.

So the Christian always lives within this Trinitarian framework of God's action – created by God the Father, redeemed by God the Son, and transformed by God the Spirit.

Transformation involves a new framework for understanding the world and ourselves as the rightful property of God. It involves the establishment of new habits, new patterns of life, new approaches to people and to circumstances. It means living 'as if' all that Christian theology says really is true: that Jesus Christ is Lord of heaven and earth, that he has risen from the dead, and therefore death is ultimately a broken, defeated enemy no longer to be feared. It means living as if Christ has died for my sins, and therefore even though I continue to commit them, ultimately they are dealt with and I need not live covered in shame. It means treating each person I meet as someone created in the likeness of God, precious and with dignity, with the potential of sharing God's nature again. It means living as if this really is a world graced with God's goodness, a world to be celebrated, protected and preserved as God's possession and gift. It means living as if I am loved, unconditionally, warmly, constantly and totally.

I once talked with a young student who was considering carefully whether to become a follower of Christ or not. He had looked closely at the reasons for and against, and found it hard to decide. There seemed good reason to believe, but then again, there was nothing absolutely conclusive about the arguments. He was stuck, not knowing which way to turn. I suggested to him that he try an experiment. For a few weeks, live as if it's really true. Pray as if God is really listening, read the Bible as if God is trying to speak to you through it, meet with other Christians as if when they gather, God is really present among them. And live not only as if you are yourself loved by God, live as if everyone you meet each day is as well. He thought this sounded reasonable and not impossible, so he agreed to give it a try.

He came back a week later. I could tell immediately that something was different. The worried frown he had worn before was transformed into a definite smile. 'I did what you said, and it worked! I started to live as if it was true; now I know it is true.' He had begun to experience transformation.

Real change

To respond to the message of the rule of God is to bring a new set of values to bear on every aspect of a person's or a community's life. The goal of evangelism must be to bring every aspect of the life of an individual or community under that rule. Unfortunately, however, sometimes the transformation that takes place is a pale imitation of this. What starts with real energy and an exciting new life ends up with just a few changed habits – going to church instead of mowing the lawn on Sunday mornings, a new set of friends, not swearing quite so much, and that's about it. Roy McCloughry points out that 'all too often in Western society, people respond to the message of the evangelist by adding a new religious "compartment" to the rest of their life'.[3] It's like building an extension to a house – the rest of the building carries on just the same as before; the only difference is a rather nice religious conservatory added on to the back, which visitors rarely see, but which can be enjoyed at weekends. If we begin to understand evangelism as an invitation to bring the whole of our life under the rule of God, then this is just plain inadequate. It has to be an invitation to transformation.

This compartmentalism often stems from a type of Christology known as 'Docetic'. The word comes from a Greek word, *dokeo*, which means to 'seem'. Docetic Christology says that Jesus only 'seemed' to be human. In reality, he was a divine being in a human shell. Several figures within early Church theology flirted dangerously with this idea. One, called Apollinarius, thought that Jesus had a human body, but his soul was not human at all – it was purely divine. We might call it a 'Mr Spock Theology' after the character in *Star Trek*, who seems human on the outside (apart from those ears), but who inside is pure Vulcan, unable to feel or understand human emotions and sensitivities.

Sadly, even though Apollinarius' views were declared heretical, there is still a lot of Docetic Christology around today, although most of those who hold it wouldn't call it this. It results in the view that being a Christian does not actually affect real life. It affects some kind of inner spiritual world, all to do with feelings and what you do on Sundays. And Jesus – this other-worldly character who drifts 18 inches above the ground and is never hungry, tired or frustrated – has precious little understanding of the real problems we have to face. Instead, as Dallas Willard puts it, he 'is thought to be concerned with some feathery realm, other than the one we must deal with, and must deal with now'.[4]

If my Jesus has very little to do with real life, then my Christian faith will have very little to do with real life. And the rest of my life will carry on pretty much as it did before, with its petty failures, shady compromises and broken promises. Being a Christian will make hardly any discernible difference to the things that occupy my mind most of the time. And this is one of the main reasons why the churches of the West are struggling today. It is not because they haven't taken on the latest management techniques, or understood postmodernism, or are technologically behind the times. It is because many of us Christians in the West today live lives that are virtually indistinguishable from those of our non-Christian friends, neighbours and work colleagues. I don't mention this to blame anyone in particular. It just seems to be true. As one young man once told me: 'The reason I cannot become a Christian is because I see no difference between the way Christians behave and the way non-Christians behave.'

Digging beneath the surface of many even apparently successful churches, it doesn't take long to discover a common feeling that our Christianity occupies a parallel universe from the rest of our lives. And the effect on evangelism is huge, as it eventually leaves Christians bored, frustrated and going through the motions. And if that's all Christian life is, then out of kindness to their non-Christian friends, they quietly ignore all the well-intentioned pleas to bring them to church.

This is far from the kind of restoration of the image of God that the New Testament, Athanasius and the fathers of Chalcedon had in mind. For them, the renewal of the divine likeness was to leave no part of a person's life untouched. Bringing our lives under God's rule, into the place where his will is done, could never be merely the addition of a religious extension to the house of our lives. It can only be the rebuilding of the house all over again, this time upon firm and solid rock. Our impoverished imagination finds it hard to make any sense of early Christian language of sharing the divine image, glory and likeness, but this is what they meant – a new kind of life, made available through Jesus, driven and inspired by God's own Spirit, bringing us into God's own being and likeness. We are intended to be god-like – nothing short of that. Not in the debased sense of unlimited capricious power and thunderous repressive authority – that's a picture more of the Greek or pagan gods, rather than the God of the Bible. Limitless power is always dangerous in the hands of those who have not learnt humility, self-sacrifice and self-control. Instead, we are to be like God in his creative love and boundless generosity. As C. S. Lewis put it: 'He is beginning to turn you into the same kind of thing as Himself. He is beginning, so to speak, to "inject" his kind of life and thought, his *Zōe* (life) into you.'[5]

No one can manage this process. Nor can any human programme make it happen. This is God's image, and only God can restore it, as Athanasius saw with crystal clarity. Yet we can create the conditions in which it can happen, just as a gardener creates the conditions for growth by ensuring good soil, adequate water and placing the plant where it will get plenty of sunshine. And churches need to attend carefully to all these things if transformation, and hence evangelism, is to take root at all. How we might do that is the subject of the next chapter. Before we end this one, however, one more important point needs to be made.

Changing places

Churches are meant to be places that can change abnormal people into normal people. People who are shadows change into real people. People who are half-dead in their addiction to destructive habits of selfishness and egotism, change into rich, fully alive human beings, knowing how to love, even when it hurts. At the same time they are also to be places that transform the life of the communities and societies around them by this very same power.

The rule of God rightfully extends not just over the Church, but over the whole of creation, and a healthy church will see that rule being enacted and highlighted all around it. As it prays for healing, people find again the physical wholeness that bears witness to God's care for us. Simple, deliberate acts of kindness, such as the opening of homes and hospitality for strangers, or establishing Christian rehabilitation centres for drug addicts, bear witness to the rule of God and involve a measure of transformation of the world, not just the Church.

We're not talking here about 'bringing the kingdom of God on earth'. This was a popular cry among some ambitious theologians and social reformers at the end of the nineteenth century, before the First World War burst the bubble of Western European hubris. Reckoning without the deep hold of our addiction to sin, they thought they could build this kingdom here with few real problems. Perhaps now we know better. A century of war, holocaust, terrorism and genocide has made us more humble, more sanguine. In a memorable scene from the end of Nikos Kazantzakis' book *The Last Temptation*, as Jesus carries his cross to Golgotha, the sick and disabled of Jerusalem pelt him with sticks, stones, even their crutches, because he had not healed them all.[6] Jesus' miracles, healings, the signs that the kingdom had come near and was available to all, were not universal. He did not banish sickness, evil and sin for ever: that is still to come. If the kingdom is to come, it will be God who brings it, not us.

Jesus' miracles were, however, a sign that these are broken powers, defeated enemies, and just occasionally we see the visible signs of their downfall. The Church as the body of Christ remains Christ's physical presence on earth, as it were, called to do what Jesus did and say what he said. Naturally, it cannot die his death or win his victory over death – but it is to follow the pattern of that death and resurrection, and it can expect God's power to heal, offer God's forgiveness and speak prophetic words of wisdom. As it does that, it sets up signs of God's rule, not only in the lives of those who acknowledge it, but also in the communities of people around who don't.

A healthy church is a transforming community in both senses. It is a community that transforms those who belong to it, loosing the hold of our addiction to sin, and replacing it with a love for what is good and healthy, every bit as much as an AA meeting tries practically to loose the hold of alcohol on its members, replacing it with something better. It also transforms the life of the community around it in slow but sure ways. And when it does these things, it begins to be evangelistic without even trying too hard.

Tragically, churches have so often seen these as competing agendas – as if we had to choose between evangelism and social commitment or personal growth. They belong together, and only work when they are together. When it begins to be itself, realizing the grandeur of its calling and the resources available to it from the Spirit, there is nothing on earth to compare with the Church of God.

Notes

1 Athanasius, *De Incarnatione*, 5.
2 Athanasius, *De Incarnatione*, 13.
3 Roy McCloughry, *The Eye of the Needle*, Leicester: IVP, 1990, p. 123.
4 Dallas Willard, *The Divine Conspiracy*, London: Fount, 1998, p. 1.
5 C. S. Lewis, *Mere Christianity*, London: Geoffrey Bles, 1952, p. 150.
6 Nikos Kazantzakis, *The Last Temptation*, London: Faber & Faber, 1975, p. 451.

CHAPTER 8

How to spot an evangelistic church

When I was a child and summer holidays came around, our family would usually pack up the car, catch a ferry, and drive to the west of Ireland. My sister and I would often sleep in the back seat as we drove across Kilkenny, Tipperary and Limerick, and wake up as we entered the small town in County Clare where we would spend the next weeks lazily on holiday with family and friends. The west coast of Ireland is a wild and bracing place. As we arrived, we would usually walk out onto the rocks by the sea, or onto one of the various headlands nearby. All the stuffiness of hot cities and dull roads would be swept away as we stood looking out onto the great Atlantic Ocean, with the wind whipping our faces and the spray reaching up from the pounding waves far below to cling to our hair, leaving the taste of fresh salt air lingering in our mouths. It felt like entering a new world. There was exhilaration as the powerful and cleansing wind blew away all the dull memories of school and city streets. There was a touch of danger as we peered over the cliffs into the turmoil of the sea far below. There was a delicious sense of anticipation as the long weeks of the summer stretched out before us. It was a world where we felt more alive and alert to everything happening around us – a world of wonder, not exactly safe and predictable, but exhilarating and energizing.

Those childhood experiences gave me an echo of what it means to enter into God's kingdom. Jesus ushered people into a new world. He invited people to enter the kingdom of God, the place where God is king and where his will is done. It too is a bracing world, not safe and predictable, but an exhilarating place where our deepest and best desires are met and where we find the love, forgiveness, significance and challenge we desperately crave. It is the kingdom in which Jesus Christ is king, and where we can find ourselves refreshed, elated, even trembling with anticipation.

The Church is meant to offer a taste of that kingdom to anyone who comes near, but how does that translate into practicalities? Jesus performed acts that became signs that the kingdom was drawing near. What are the signs to look for in an ordinary local church that give a taste of the kingdom?

Jesus transformed people. He brought them into a whole new way of relating to the world around them. This chapter looks at five key relationships in which our lives consist, and that determine the kind of people we are. It also examines how they change under the rule of God, and how churches might see them as signs of the kingdom to which they point. They are:

- A new relationship with God – Adoration
- A new relationship with others – Belonging
- A new relationship with creation – Compassion
- A new relationship with the self – Discipleship
- A new relationship with words – Evangelism

A new relationship with God – Adoration

Jesus invited people into the kingdom of God. And that meant learning to order their lives afresh under God's rule. So, churches will need to be places that start by fostering a new relationship with God.

How to spot an evangelistic church

This may sound obvious, but it's surprising how easy it is for churches to miss this simple point. Churches can become consumed with the techniques of management, the demands of technology or even the minutiae of liturgical correctness, and somehow miss out on the cultivation of intimacy, awe and adoration of God. It's possible to go to some churches for many years, gain a fine understanding of theology and church politics, but to be no closer to the God of Jesus Christ than you were at the start.

The culture of the West at the start of the third millennium longs for intimacy. Our culture's obsession with constant communication by any means possible, whether e-mail, text messages, mobile phones, chat rooms or online communities testifies to our inability to be alone, our desperate need to be in touch, to share secrets and lives. Our fascination with sex also points to the same thing; as Douglas Coupland put it: 'Starved for affection, terrified of abandonment, I began to wonder if sex was really just an excuse to look deeply into another human being's eyes.'[1] Although there is a desperately sad side to this inability to be alone, at the same time it reflects a basic human need – for intimacy. Without it we shrivel and hide. And this desire for intimacy with each other is again a vague echo of our need for intimacy with God our creator:

> earnestly I seek you;
> my soul thirsts for you,
> my body longs for you,
> in a dry and weary land
> where there is no water. (Psalm 63.1)

One place where Christians have always looked to cultivate a closer, more fulfilled and intimate relationship with

God, as well as a keen sense of awe, has been in the act of worship. So the question of what a church does when it gathers together week by week has a large bearing upon its ability to usher people into a new relationship with God.

New Testament worship took a variety of forms, and it's not always easy to figure out quite what it looked like. One of the best descriptions comes in an early letter in Paul's correspondence with the church in Corinth:

> So if the whole church comes together and everyone speaks in tongues, and some who do not understand or some unbelievers come in, will they not say that you are out of your mind? But if an unbeliever or someone who does not understand comes in while everybody is prophesying, he will be convinced by all that he is a sinner and will be judged by all, and the secrets of his heart will be laid bare. So he will fall down and worship God, exclaiming, 'God is really among you!' What then shall we say, brothers? When you come together, everyone has a hymn, or a word of instruction, a revelation, a tongue or an interpretation. All of these must be done for the strengthening of the church. (1 Corinthians 14.23–26)

One quality in particular stands out in this description: that Christian worship was *dynamic*. It's interesting to note in passing that New Testament churches expected unbelieving visitors to drop in on their meetings, and one of the questions that governed what they did there is how such people would react. Whatever we decide about the controversial issue of tongues in worship, it's clear from this passage that what these early Christians did together had a dramatic effect. An ordinary, inquisitive

Corinthian pagan is invited into the Christian meeting. While there, he is unable to escape the powerful sense that God is really and tangibly present, and exclaims, 'God is really among you!' Paul expects that as Christians meet together, God can be experienced as truly present, even by those who come in without any Christian faith at all!

Whether Paul means prophecy in the 'charismatic' sense experienced in many churches today, or a prophetic quality in preaching – which is able to hit the nail on the head, saying just what needs to be said at a particular time – the effect is that 'the secrets of his heart [are] laid bare'. Most Christians will recall times when a word in a sermon, a song, a 'word of knowledge' or prophetic word has penetrated right down to the depths of their being. This might be called 'inspired communication', which is perhaps a useful simple definition of prophecy. When it happens, it's as if you are seen through, understood, and the secrets which no one else knows are addressed and resolved by a word from someone who couldn't possibly have known what was in your heart. It's this kind of thing that Paul has in mind. Worship and preaching that address the 'secrets of the heart', that go beyond the intellectual and rational, that have a numinous quality, bring a sense of the presence of the true God. They transform the singing of hymns and the saying of prayers into acts of true adoration of the living God.

This kind of worship has that slightly dangerous, risky quality which we mentioned earlier as important for transformative churches. Paul expects worship to be provocative. No one could leave a meeting of the Corinthian church remarking that it was boring or dull. When is the last time you sensed danger in going to church – that you were going to meet with the living God, to become acutely aware of his presence and power? It's not surprising when this happens that people sometimes tremble, laugh, raise hands to heaven or even dance. When the secrets of the heart are gently exposed and quietly answered, all kinds of responses are possible. Yet so often church doesn't feel like this. It's a tragedy that at a time when many people in the West are searching for spiritual reality, churches are often the last places they would expect to find a genuinely spiritual encounter with the God of creation and redemption.

This kind of worship doesn't necessarily have to be loud and dramatic. Quiet contemplative services, reverent ritual, or thoughtful, perceptive informal teaching can all do the same – the main thing is not so much the style but the spirit of expectancy for God's reality and presence that it carries. This expectancy arises out of a life of prayer at other times in the week, a sense of anticipation that God will make himself known, and an understanding of worship that sees it primarily as response to God, not a performance for him.

Worship that carries this dynamic quality cannot fail to engender a deeper sense of the reality and holiness of God, a stronger sense of intimacy, awe and adoration, which are vital foundations for a life transformed under the rule of God. It cannot help but foster a richer spirituality out of which evangelism flows, as others are invited into the friendship with God that Christians have begun to know.

A new relationship with others – Belonging

Jesus brought people into new relationship with others. We have already noticed the strong indications in the Gospels that he intended small communities of disciples, centred upon himself and the life of the kingdom, to continue after his ascension. Paul subsequently envisaged churches in which the normal barriers in first-century Greco-Roman society (between Gentiles and Jews, women and men, free men and slaves) were simply irrelevant. A church modelled on the kingdom of God will be able to draw people into new patterns of relationship with each other, based on an appreciation of the value of every person.

Personal and spiritual growth normally happens not in isolation but in relationship. We tend to change when we see a quality in someone else that we admire and would like to emulate, and we learn to exercise that quality as we see someone else live it out. Embodied truth is much more effective than disembodied concepts. So relationships are vital for transformation, and a transforming church needs to place a high premium on the quality of its relationships.

Corinthian worship was not only dynamic; it was also *interactive*. Like a large bring-and-share lunch, where the thing only works if everyone brings something slightly different to share with everyone else, each person was expected to bring their own special contribution to the gathering. No one was passive, idle, simply a spectator. Instead, each had something to offer and to receive, whether 'a hymn, or a word of instruction, a revelation, a tongue or an interpretation'.

Sitting in church, I sometimes wonder what would happen if the minister didn't turn up one morning. Imagine they forgot, or slept through the alarm. Many churches would simply panic. Without a minister, who will lead? Who will preach, or administer the sacraments, or give the notices? Some might just cancel the service, some might muddle through somehow; in many, church couldn't function without a 'minister'. Now this isn't to denigrate the role of ordained ministers – they have a

127

definite and vital role to play in church life. Yet it is to point up the level of dependency many churches have on those who lead the church. As a result, a visitor who had never been to church before would be forgiven for thinking those in the pews are expected to be passive recipients of sermons or sacraments, while those at the front do all the work – miles away from what Paul taught the Corinthians to do.

An example of churchly passivity is the traditional sermon. Did the early Christians preach sermons? Did Paul? On a visit to Troas, he spoke long into the night at a church meeting. The occasion caused a bit of a stir (it's told in Acts 20) when one young Christian called Eutychus nodded off to sleep during the talk (evidence by the way that Paul wasn't the most riveting of speakers, and an encouragement to all preachers who have seen their congregations doze a little). The boy fell out of the window and was killed, yet was restored to life by God through Paul's prayers. The narrative tells us that Paul 'kept on talking until midnight' (Acts 20.7) and then after the incident with Eutychus, that he even kept talking until daylight (20.11).

Does this mean Paul's sermons lasted several hours? Yes and no. Luke the author of Acts uses two specific words for Paul's speech as he tells the story. One is the Greek word *dialegomai*, which more accurately means 'discuss', and from which we get our word 'dialogue'. It seems that in fact Paul was not speaking *at* them, but talking *with* them, discussing, answering questions and expecting interaction.

The impression is strengthened by the second word, used in verse 11, *homileō*, which means 'talk with'. Earlier in his two-part narrative, when Luke told the story of the married couple discussing recent events in

Jerusalem on their way to Emmaus after the first Easter weekend, he uses the same word to describe their conversation (Luke 24.14). Again it is a word more at home in the context of dialogue rather than monologue. Paul's teaching, here at least, was interactive. He did not tend to give 20-minute speeches before the final hymn.

Again, the purpose of this is not to recommend the abolition of the sermon. It is, however, to point out that the sermon is perhaps more of a cultural construct than we tend to think. Christian and biblical teaching is essential to a healthy church, as we shall see, yet the way it was delivered in the earliest churches was probably much more interactive than it is in most of ours.[2] If they want to encourage a sense of ownership, participation and involvement, one area of experimentation for Christian leaders and preachers is the sermon. Interactive sermons are more risky and unpredictable than the monologue, yet handled skilfully and well prepared, they may lead to better communication, greater interest and more relevant application. They need not compromise the authority of the Bible, but might enable a greater sense of the Christian community gathered round the text. In the right contexts and on the right occasions, sermons with time for questions, or opportunity for discussion and feedback, are worth trying.

Members of churches in New Testament times were expected to be active participants, not passive recipients. Such churches were places where each person was understood as having been gifted by God with something unique and valuable for the well-being of the whole church. The problems in Corinth seem to have stemmed in large measure from a group who felt that they were the only ones who were truly gifted or were worth listening to.[3] A church with a consumer mentality, where the laity are purely passive consumers of whatever is delivered from the front, will rarely be an evangelistic church. However, a church where members are brought into new relationships, where they are seen as gifted both to give and receive care, attention, forgiveness and love, just as they have received from God, will be an energizing and attractive community. It will provoke questions, especially in a culture that has lost the power to create a shared life, one in which there is little sense of commonality, but instead atomized individualism, and isolated and uninvolved lives.

From time to time, the Church has recovered its true identity as community. For example, the Reformation doctrine of the 'priesthood of all believers' was a reaction to a Church dominated by clergy as the possessors and dispensers of everything that mattered. It was essentially a reaffirmation of the insight that every believer had the responsibility to stand in the place of Christ to offer counsel, reassurance and wisdom to everyone else in the Church. The question this poses local churches is whether they see themselves primarily as institutions or communities, as programme-centred or people-centred. In the next chapter we will look at patterns of leadership and how church might be structured to create this sense of belonging and mutual care. At the moment, the main point is that a church that reflects the life of the kingdom will have a clear aim of bringing people into relationship with one another, where they can give and receive care and instruction, rather than maintaining the strongly hierarchical top-down structure that many churches have at present. Churches that are effective evangelistically are usually at the same time places where people can find new relationships, where they are valued for what they bring as well as receiving care from others.

A new relationship with creation – Compassion

Jesus' kingdom touched not just the lives of individuals, but spoke of a renewed creation, a renovation of the created order fractured at the fall. Storms – symbols of chaos and disorder within the Old Testament – were stilled as Jesus the King uttered a word of command. Water, which threatened to drown anyone who fell into it, became supportive and co-operative as the Son of God stepped out of a boat. Inadequate food was multiplied so that the hungry could eat, be satisfied, and 12 baskets were left over. Malformed limbs straightened out, and lifelong illnesses vanished at a stroke. In the ministry of Jesus, disease and death were temporarily banished to the far corners of hell where they truly belonged.

The miracles of Jesus were not arbitrary demonstrations of his power, or even illustrations of his teaching. They were signs that God was now coming as king, and that his enemies were in retreat. Creation was being healed and signs of the final reordering of the world were visible: 'Jesus went throughout Galilee, teaching in their synagogues, preaching the good news of the kingdom, and healing every disease and sickness among the people' (Matthew 4.23).

Paul also understood this point, seeing the pain of the created order, longing for its final release:

The creation waits in eager expectation for the sons of God to be revealed. For the creation was subjected to frustration, not by its own choice, but by the will of the one who subjected it, in hope that the creation itself will be liberated from its bondage to decay and brought into the glorious freedom of the

children of God. We know that the whole creation
has been groaning as in the pains of childbirth right
up to the present time. (Romans 8.19–22)

A church that wants to be like Jesus and to reflect the life
of his kingdom will therefore be involved in some way in
the restoration of creation. Just as Jesus did, it will set up
signs that one day God will restore order to this fractured
world, and end creation's bondage to decay.

When a church proclaims that Jesus is Lord, that God
is in charge of his world, a likely response from anyone
aware of the harsh realities of life is, to quote John
McEnroe, 'You cannot be serious!' The world certainly
doesn't look much like a world under the control of a
good and loving God. The difficult question is quite a
reasonable one: 'If your God is really in charge of this
world, what is he doing about cancer, about the homeless, about AIDS or poverty?' It is the age-old problem
of suffering, and usually Christians have sprung to the
defence of God with the science of apologetics, mounting careful and thoughtful intellectual answers. Some of
these convince, some don't. And they often don't in the
context of real suffering. We're back with our problem of
disembodied truth, which doesn't cut much ice either in
postmodern culture or the experience of pain.

If a church is doing nothing about these things, then
however cogent and clever its apologetic answers to the
problem of suffering, they will all sound a little hollow
and just a touch smug. It is vital that Christians can
mount an explanation of the existence of suffering in a
world that they claim to be basically good and under the
rule of a thoroughly good God. Yet perhaps the most
effective answer to the question of what God is doing
about suffering is the answer Philip gave to Nathanael:
'Come and see!' (John 1.46).

What is God doing about pain in his world? He is calling people like you and me to be transformed into the kind of people who are part of the solution rather than part of the problem. He is gathering a community of people who are involved in the healing of creation, who out of their joy at knowing a good God who has graced their lives, are busy gracing the lives of others, visiting those with cancer, touching those with AIDS, giving time and money to those who are poor, praying for the healing of those who are sick, cleaning up local landscapes ravaged by vandalism. Unlike Thor or Jupiter, the God of the Bible doesn't send too many thunderbolts. He normally does his work through things, and especially through people. He worked the salvation of the world through Jesus, and he fights against evil and pain through people who live under his rule.

But of course this answer only has credibility if it is actually true, and you can point people to a local church community where it is happening! Commitment to acts of care and compassion are not optional extras for churches that want to be evangelistic; they are indispensable. A provocative church that reflects the kingdom of God will demonstrate what happens when Christ's lordship is enacted. Under God's rule, the sick find healing, the suffering find comfort, and the lost find welcome.

If the ministry of Jesus pointed forward to the healing of creation, then a local church that wants to be in step with that will need to look carefully at its particular part of creation and ask, 'What needs healing here?' Is it loneliness, homelessness, boredom, the environment, poverty or aimlessness? Naturally, few churches can address all the social problems surrounding them, but with prayer, discernment, a little research and energy, most churches can alight on some ministry in their local area that can become a powerful sign that God is concerned for his creation and has not given up on it.

One inner-city church put aside a weekend and many pots of paint to brighten up a dank, urine-soaked subway nearby, inviting local residents to join in, and generating no small stir in the area. In a wealthy area, another church youth group put on a concert and performed music in a local shopping mall to raise money not for themselves or their church, but to enable the digging of a well in a village in Nigeria. A group of Christian students borrowed their college's dining hall, and invited their friends to a simple African meal with music, yet charging them a high price, so that the profits could go towards the rebuilding of educational prospects for young black South Africans.

These things can be done not for effect or to impress, but just because they were the kind of things Jesus did. They are the kind of things that happen in the kingdom of God – creation is renewed, the thirsty are given water, the poor are given hope. Actions like these have their own integrity as a sign of God's rule. Although not performed for evangelistic effect, the inevitable result is that when it comes to direct evangelism, such churches tend to find it works better. There is a clearer sense of what people are being invited into, and of the kind of life that Christian faith involves.

A new relationship with the self – Discipleship

When people met Jesus, they were never quite the same again. Whether it was Zacchaeus' radically new attitude to his wealth; the demon-possessed man from Gadara who was restored to sanity and belonging; or Peter, a fisherman who became a leader of the church in one of the centres of the empire; Jesus changed people, and they began to see themselves very differently. We have discussed already the need for churches to be communities that are capable of transforming people into the image of Christ. This, however, needs to be more than a pious aspiration.

Perhaps the main way in which Christians' lives and minds are shaped in church life is through the regular diet of preaching and teaching that they receive. In transforming churches, teaching will aim to give people two things – a theological framework that gradually reshapes their view of God, the world and themselves, and practical strategies to develop the kind of qualities of the person who lives under the rule of God. It will regularly return to the Church's main text for personal and communal transformation, the Bible itself as it describes life under the rule of God. It will encourage a careful reading of the Scriptures, the vision of life they give and the particular points at which that vision cuts against the surrounding culture.

In line with modern business practice, many churches now have mission statements. Very often these are so general and vague that they mean very little. Imagine, however, a church that had as its mission statement 'to teach ordinary people how to love God and love their neighbour'. It's not a bad description of life under the rule of God, and sets a very practical agenda for a local church. Dallas Willard writes:

Imagine if you can, discovering in your church newsletter or bulletin an announcement of a six-week seminar on how genuinely to bless someone who is spitting on you . . . Or suppose the announced seminar was on how to live without purposely indulged lust or covetousness. Or how to quit condemning

the people around you. Or how to be free of anger
and all its complications. Imagine, also, a guarantee
that at the end of the seminar, those who have done
the prescribed studies and exercises will actually be
able to bless those who are spitting on them and so
on . . . When you teach children or adults to ride a
bicycle or swim, they actually do ride bikes or swim
on appropriate occasions. You don't just teach them
that they *ought* to ride bicycles, or that it is *good* to
ride bicycles, or that they should be ashamed if they
don't.[4]

However such a programme might work in practice,
these imaginings highlight the need for practical help in
developing a style of life in harmony with God's rule.
Churches of the kingdom will tend to measure success
not only by the numbers of people coming, or even converted, but by the level of change visible in the lives of
those who belong. Disciples need disciplines. Not usually
punitive or corrective discipline, but practical strategies
of prayer, meditation, action and theology which in the
long run produce change of character.[5]

A new relationship with words – Evangelism

Finally, we come to evangelism itself. And we do so deliberately. Jesus did not simply perform signs of the coming kingdom; he explained them, and invited people to
enter it. So far we have been thinking about growing
churches that provoke questions. The other side of the
coin is having the ability to answer them. The Church on
the day of Pentecost was provocative enough to make
people ask, 'What does this mean?' It was also alert and
astute enough to enable Peter to get up and explain. The

confusion of language at Babel was reversed as people heard God's invitation in their own tongue. Peter's words themselves then became vehicles of invitation from God to kingdom life.

Few churches are growing today that do not have some kind of group for those enquiring about the Christian faith. There are exceptions, but most churches seem to need some forum where Christian faith can be explained in appropriate words, where enquirers can ask questions about it and hear some answers to those questions. Alpha is clearly the best-known of these and has proved a brilliant vehicle for people of all backgrounds, nationalities and perspectives to explore the questions they bring.

Such courses for enquirers are ideal ways to enable people to experience the life of the kingdom, enable a church to answer the questions and to put the kingdom into words. Yet as we have seen, they need to be understood as part of a wider theology of the Church and the kingdom rather than just the answer on their own to church growth. Many churches have found Alpha works well. Some have found that it doesn't. The problem may lie less with the course than with the church. Churches that already in some measure display the characteristics of the kingdom outlined above will tend to find evangelistic courses naturally producing new disciples of Christ. Churches where the worship is dull and uninviting, where there is little sense of mutual care, no discernible concern for the locality and no one is experiencing personal transformation, may well find that such courses do them little good. Words that correspond with reality are rich and fruitful; words that don't are hollow.

Doing evangelism in a church, speaking the words of invitation to life under God's rule, is a little bit like putting your foot on the accelerator of a car. Things happen, but *what* happens all depends on what gear you're in. If a church is in fourth gear, so to speak – it's a good healthy positive place to be with the kind of characteristics mentioned above – then an evangelistic mission or a course will tend to reap quite a harvest. If it's in first or second gear – with some of the above, but not all, and only in small measure – then it may see some growth, but not much. If it's in reverse gear, with suspicion, jealousy, dissent and pride everywhere, then engaging in evangelism will probably make things worse not better. I have been involved in a few church missions where the evangelistic effort served only to bring to the surface all kinds of tension, mistrust and frustration that had lain smouldering and hidden for many years. I've also been on many others where the mission enabled a natural expression of what God was doing in the church already, with many people drawn to a new faith in Christ as they were attracted to this community, which appeared to them to have something different, something special.

Jesus brought people into new relationships with God, others, creation, with themselves and with words. These new relationships are characteristic of churches that live under the rule of God, churches that provoke the question and are evangelistic in their very being. This kind of agenda may require a radical rethink of a church's programme and priorities. It is notoriously harder to close something down in church life than start it up.

One church held an annual meeting, which they called the 'Ichabod meeting'. Ichabod was the name of one of the sons of Phinehas, a priest in early Israel at the time when the Philistines captured the Ark of the Covenant (1 Samuel 4.21). His mother gave him this gloomy name, meaning 'the glory of the Lord has departed'. The purpose of this meeting was to ask a straightforward question: 'From which of our church's activities has God's glory departed?' In other words, were there groups, activities, meetings, committees that no longer contributed to the church's vision of where it was going? If there were, then hard decisions needed to be made, and resources rearranged.

Churches are often far too busy doing far too many things, and as a result do few of them well. As this chapter closes, it may help to offer a number of key questions a church might ask itself to test its own relationship to the kingdom.

- Adoration – Do regular members find that Sunday worship feeds their own spiritual life, enabling them to draw close to God and taste both intimacy and awe?
- Belonging – Is there a structure within which every member of the church can give and receive care? Do most people feel they have a contribution to make, or are they mainly passive recipients?
- Compassion – Does the church do anything that expresses practical effective concern for its local community? Is it appropriate for the needs of that community and the resources of the church?
- Discipleship – Is there a structure that enables Christians to be accountable to each other for their growth? Does teaching give practical strategies for developing life under God's rule?
- Evangelism – Does the church have a place for searchers to explore and ask questions – Alpha or something similar?

Building a church like this is not always easy. To build these characteristics into church life takes time, sensitivity, humility and not a little skill. In short, it needs wise leadership. And that is what the next chapter will explore.

Notes

1 Douglas Coupland, *Life after God*, London: Simon & Schuster, 1994, p. 125.

2 An interesting account of what early church meetings might have looked like is found in: Robert Banks, *Going to Church in the First Century: An Eyewitness Account*, Beaumont: Christian, 1990.

3 For further reading on this wider point, see: Gerd Theissen, *The Social Setting of Pauline Christianity*, Studies of the New Testament and its World, ed. John Riches, Edinburgh: T&T Clark, 1982, chs 2, 3 and 4; also Graham Tomlin, *The Power of the Cross: Theology and the Death of Christ in Paul, Luther and Pascal*, Paternoster Biblical and Theological Monographs, Carlisle: Paternoster, 1999, part I.

4 Dallas Willard, *The Divine Conspiracy*, London: Fount, 1998, p. 344.

5 For approaches to this task see Graham Tomlin, *The Seven Deadly Sins and How to Overcome Them*, Oxford: Lion Hudson, 2007.

CHAPTER 9

Leading evangelistic churches

The evangelistic guest service had been a disappointment. The appeal had succeeded in getting only the two or three people who always made new commitments on these occasions to come forward. The speaker was obviously a bit upset that there seemed so few genuine non-church people present, but of course he was too polite to say so. The minister muttered some apologies as he put the speaker on the train, and drove home feeling resentful. He'd done his job in getting the speaker there. Why hadn't his people done their job in bringing their friends and neighbours? Why were they so sleepy and unconcerned? How could he motivate them for evangelism? How could he begin to help the church grow? Why wasn't it working? Was it them, or him? What was he doing wrong?

Guiding and empowering churches is often a struggle. Yet I am increasingly convinced that when it comes to evangelism, the real issue in our churches is not so much motivation as leadership. On visits to churches to speak on evangelism, I have sometimes asked the simple question, 'Would you like your friends or family who are not yet Christians to become Christians?' The answer is almost always a heartfelt 'Yes'. Most Christians think of their faith as something positive and valuable, and want others to share it too, sometimes desperately so. The problem is knowing how. It's not that they are not motivated to see this happen; it's just that evangelism has often been made to seem so difficult and complicated that

141

they don't know where to start. And this is where leadership comes in.

The quality and style of leadership in any church is a vital aspect of its survival, let alone its growth. Some statistics suggest that every Sunday in North America and Western Europe, the staggering figure of 53,000 people walk out of church and never come back. And for many of them, it is the style of leadership that is the telling factor. Clerical leadership that fails to recognize the issues real people face, that is either over-dogmatic or lacks direction, or that stifles the initiative and flair of lay people is deeply frustrating and, sooner or later, will alienate some people to the point where they see little point in continuing turning up. It is said in business circles that 'people don't leave jobs, they leave managers'. And much the same is true in church.[1]

So leadership matters. Yet when we start talking practicalities of leadership, evangelism and church growth, some people get nervous, for two main reasons. Influenced by business technique and management theory, it isn't hard to draft 'ten-stage plans to ensure growth in your church', or sure-fire, quick-fix solutions – try this method/evangelism programme/gospel outline and your church is guaranteed to grow! It's not that business and management theory have no place in church or are devoid of wisdom. Churches can be a touch naïve, and some hard-headed advice from those who know the dynamics of human organizations can save a lot of heartache and pain. It's just that these are not the last word in the kingdom of God. God's rule works in different ways from human kingdoms, and that always needs to be kept in mind when using secular techniques.

The other reason is that leadership is not easy in our times. Contemporary culture is tainted by a deep suspicion of the nature and role of power within societies and institutions. Authority figures such as doctors, teachers, academics, politicians and clergy are no longer assumed to have our best interests at heart. Unconsciously schooled by postmodern mistrust of truth and power, we are taught endlessly to suspect and to question those who wield power over us.[2] Now some of this has to be good. There are those who would abuse the trust placed in them, and any society has to be alert and watchful for them. However, among doctors, clergy, teachers and politicians, a constant refrain sounds: that of low morale and disillusionment. Denied the financial rewards of business or financial management, seldom thanked when they do well, they feel under constant suspicion, waiting for the ton of bricks to land on their heads when they make a mistake. You cannot build a society on suspicion and mistrust.

We live in a culture caught between suspicion of authority and the need for trust. In this context, Christian leadership needs to be careful to avoid the tendency to mechanistic manipulation or the suspicion of power. For centuries, clergy and Christian leaders have been used to being treated and seeing themselves as authority figures, bolstered by the *imprimatur* of the voice of Church or Bible, to which all must defer and listen. Perhaps this was never a good biblical way of looking at it anyway, but no longer can we sustain such a view, for both theological and cultural reasons. Perhaps the image we need for Christian leadership today is not so much that of a headmaster or president, nor even those of servant or shepherd, somewhat out of place in an egalitarian, mainly urban society, but that of a gardener.

Growth in the kingdom

In God's kingdom, growth belongs to God and not to us. No person or method can guarantee growth in a church.

Sometimes, you do all the right things, yet for some mysterious reason, growth doesn't come. It's significant that many of Jesus' parables of the kingdom were agricultural. In Matthew 13 we find a collection of Jesus' stories designed to help his hearers understand the significance of the kingdom. Each one is about growth. The parables of the sower, the seed planted in the field and the mustard seed all breathe the world of farmers, patience and dependence. Even the parable of the yeast in the flour speaks of growth and its nurture.

The point being made here is that the life of the kingdom has a dynamic all of its own. You cannot force it to come. It comes of its own accord. The kingdom takes root, grows and flowers in a person's life, a community, a church, and this is God's work. Yet at the same time, there is a human factor in each of these stories. A farmer scatters seeds all around him; another sows good seed in a field, even though an enemy sows weeds among them; another man takes a grain of mustard seed and plants it in his solitary patch of land; a woman places yeast in the dough, and kneads it thoroughly until it is worked through the whole batch.

God makes things grow. He nurtures both biological and spiritual life in people, and it is the task of those who wish to co-operate with him, not to make things grow, but to try not to hinder their growth. In one sense the task of Christian leadership simply is to get out of the way and stop messing things up for God! Leadership in the kingdom of God is about creating the right conditions for growth, and this requires a very different mentality from thinking that you can generate the growth of the kingdom by the application of particular techniques.

The classic New Testament example of a church fixated on technique was the one based in Corinth. A

significant group within that church seem to have felt
that its fortunes depended on the tricks of Greco-Roman
rhetoric (the 'words of human wisdom' or 'eloquence' of
1 Corinthians 1.17 and 2.1), the possession of an impressive leader (1.11–12) and a good social standing
with the wider society (1.26–27). Perhaps Paul was
thinking of Jesus' parables of the kingdom when he
wrote to the Corinthians that while he had planted the
seed of their faith and Apollos had watered it, neither
was responsible for its growth – that was purely down
to God (3.5–9). Paul viewed the Christian community
in Corinth not in mechanical but organic terms. It was
not a piece of machinery to be tweaked, manipulated or
cranked up to generate power. It was 'God's field' (3.9),
in which things grew all by themselves. His and Apollos'
role (complementary, not competitive) was to provide the
conditions in which growth could take place, by planting, watering, tending and waiting.

So how do we translate this into helping provocative,
kingdom-focused, evangelistic churches to grow? In
spring, the front of our house is suddenly brought to life
by a rampant, beautiful purple-flowered clematis. I remember planting and nurturing it during its early days.
I am no great gardener, but I soon learnt I had to do two
things to help this thing grow. First, I needed to create
a structure that would help it flourish. Without something to cling to, clematis (apparently) grows straggly
and wild. I had to put in some hard, back-breaking hours
to clear from the ground various untidy and ugly plants
that had taken root there, and then fix a carefully chosen
trellis, supported by stakes in just the right places. The
second step was to give the plant a chance to thrive. We
planted a few strands of the clematis, watered them regularly, kept an eye out for weeds and pests, and waited.

Growth was slow, but gradually it came. The plant still needs careful cutting back each year (I'm sometimes pretty careless at this, but somehow it keeps growing despite me) and much of the year it doesn't show many flowers, but when it does, it is stunning to see.

Churches are like plants. They too need both structure and conditions that give them a chance to grow. This chapter looks at the structure and conditions that allow God's kingdom life to grow within a church, drawing individuals and communities to what God is doing there.

Structure

In the past, churches have often seemed the last bastions of hierarchical power. Everything was frequently concentrated in the hands of the clergy or powerful interest groups within the laity and, as we have seen before, the average lay member of the church settled down for a life of undisturbed passivity while others got on with 'running the church'. Leaders tend to get the kind of followers they want. If clergy encourage lay people to be passive, that's precisely what they will be. John Drane comments:

> Closed church structures of the kind where the leaders' main role is to take all the decisions about what needs to be done, and then carry them through themselves, will tend to stymie effective mobilization of our human resources. Because of rapid changes in our culture this structure is becoming less and less capable of doing anything at all, but inasmuch as it can be made to work, it is geared up for maintenance, not mission. It is virtually impossible for a church organized this way to be a church with mission at the centre.[3]

Rigid hierarchies will stifle growth and encourage passive consumerism. Bearing in mind what we have already seen about the need for churches to involve an active membership and a transforming culture, churches will need to have a much more dispersed exercise of power and a more relational style of structure to allow this to happen. And leaders will need both a deep sense of their own personal security in Christ and a strong dose of humility to allow this to happen.

Selling cells

Over the past few decades many churches have experimented with various types of small groups in church life. From the 1960s to the 1980s, many churches developed fellowship or home groups, which effectively were optional gatherings for church members who were committed enough to give another night a week to church activities. It was, and remains, unusual to find a church with more than 30 per cent of its Sunday worshippers regularly attending such groups. More recently, a more radical approach to small groups has gathered pace. In one version of this – the 'cell church' model – the basic unit of church life is understood not as the gathered Sunday congregation, but the small group. Normally meeting in a home, the small group effectively acts as a small church unit, providing an intimate context for worship, the application of Christian teaching to real-life issues, mutual care and encouragement, growth in discipleship, the exercise of spiritual gifts, accountability and evangelism. These groups then come together on Sundays for a meeting that will often provide the central teaching and sacramental functions of the church as a whole.[4]

Another version is what is described as 'home churches'. These are small units of church life that are deliberately multigenerational, informal, self-regulating and spontaneous. Unlike cell churches, each home church is not seen as part of a larger church – home churches tend to be independent of each other – although several home churches in a given area may come together from time to time.[5] Another structure is that of 'pastorates' – slightly larger gatherings of around 30 people who meet fortnightly to worship, study, pray, minister to one another in different ways, with the members meeting in small groupings of around three to five in the intervening weeks.

These approaches to church life, each of which have proved very effective for both discipleship and evangelism, are fascinating examples of some of the principles we've been exploring in this book. First, they operate with a much more dispersed view of authority and power than many more traditional churches. Each small group is given the dignity and responsibility to 'be church' in its local area, for its members to minister to one another, to engage in evangelism and to worship God. Leaders of cells are encouraged to take responsibility for the life of the cell under their charge, as it is effectively a small church within the supportive structure of the wider body of Christ.

Second, 'cells' draw people into intimate relationships within which personal and spiritual growth can take place. The emphasis on small groups does this far more effectively than a fixed diet of meetings in larger congregations. In some churches, it is possible to attend Sunday worship for many years before anyone will ask whether you ever pray, how you are progressing in your faith, or whether there is anything that needs to be talked over or prayed through in your life. Large congregational meetings tend to be good arenas for teaching and celebration; they don't tend to be very good for accountability and intimacy. The smaller group provides a context for the kind of intimate trust and focused ministry that both cultivates discipleship and enables evangelism.

We saw in the previous chapter the need for churches to have a strong, participative culture. Every member of a cell or pastorate is expected to be an active member. Whereas in the congregational setting, the only opportunities for lay contribution tend to be reading the lesson, taking the collection, or bringing forward the bread and wine for Communion, in the smaller setting there is regular opportunity to pray for other group members, to exercise spiritual gifts of discernment or knowledge for the benefit of others, to bring experiences of grace, and offer words of advice for others in the group who need help. In this context, the type of bring-and-share worship envisaged by Paul in Corinth, where everyone brings something to edify everyone else, suddenly becomes feasible.

Third is the particular approach to evangelism adopted in some cell churches. One big difference from the older fellowship group model is that 'cells' are intended to be evangelistic, whereas fellowship groups were primarily for Bible study and pastoral care. From this basis of a strong sense of shared life, mutual accountability and learning together, cell members are encouraged to invite those who are not yet Christians to experience the life of Christ in the small group. When they come, the group does not do anything different from their normal agenda – in most cell churches there is no such thing as an evangelistic cell meeting, because the assumption is that, just as in the Corinthian worship we examined in the previous chapter, the experience of worship, mutual care and practical learning has its own dynamism and attraction. As William Beckham comments, when a non-Christian guest is present,

... the meeting format should not be changed to convert them or to focus on them. They should be allowed to sit and watch God at work in his people ... The New Testament church knew the most powerful witness was the community of believers living in the presence, power and purpose of Christ ... through the imperfection of Christians, God reveals his power to those who observe.[6]

Beckham tells the story of a cell meeting that forgot this. A Buddhist friend of one of the members had been invited to the group. Soon after the meeting began, the Christians all turned their evangelistic guns on the poor Buddhist, and the meeting soon descended into a slanging match about religion. The man went away rather bruised, never came again, and who can blame him? Beckham's comment is apt – the mistake the group made was that 'the conversion of this one man became the focus of the meeting, not Christ'.[7] When operating as it can, the life of the cell itself provokes the question, creates desire and, in the pattern we have seen so often already, provides the context for evangelism to take place. Here is a model of church life where the focus is not evangelism, but Christ and his kingdom life. When that is in its proper place and order, evangelism tends to flow naturally from it.

Conditions

Besides a good structure, churches, like plants, also need the right conditions to enable growth to take place. Many church leaders have spent many an hour fretting over how to train their church members for evangelism, and there is no shortage of material on offer. Training packages tend to lean in one direction or another. One type focuses on apologetics, often identifying the most common topics that come up in discussion, and equipping Christians to answer questions such as the problem of suffering, whether or not other religions lead to God, or the proof for the existence of God. The other type will teach a short gospel outline which sums up the essentials of Christian faith in a few easy steps. These often come with easy-to-remember diagrams to be scribbled on the back of a napkin over a meal, with Bible verses attached.

It's easy to ridicule such things, but they do have their place. The kind of apologetic problems encountered are real, and answers are increasingly vital – modernist rationalism with its sometimes vicious critique of faith is far from dead in Western culture. It's also part of a maturing faith to have faced and answered such difficulties to one's own satisfaction, even before being able to explain some answers to others. It's easy to be snobbish about gospel outlines as well, but as a means of helping younger (and sometimes older) Christians grasp the basics of their own faith, they can be very useful indeed.

The difficulty comes in the assumption that every Christian should be articulate and intelligent enough to be able to grasp and explain complex ideas lucidly and persuasively. In the hands of those with persuasive evangelistic gifts, gospel outlines can be a natural and accessible means of explaining Christian faith. On the lips of well-intentioned Christians whose gifts really don't lie in this area, they can also sound like crass sales patter from an inexperienced used-car salesman. There are many excellent Christians who are brilliantly gifted in hospitality, listening, practical care or administration, yet who when asked to explain their faith get tongue-tied and nervous. They also tend to feel quite disabled by the expectation that any Christian worth their salt will be a capable apologist or evangelist.

So where do we go from here? How do we create the conditions for growth without falling into the perils of artificial technique? In line with the approach to evangelism we have been exploring here, leaders need to encourage three important features in the Christians in their churches:

- Living public Christian lives
- Telling personal stories
- Issuing an invitation.

A true story may help understand how this works.

A man living in a relatively affluent area (let's call him Simon) once noticed his neighbour looking a little crestfallen. He stopped to ask why, and was told the sad story. The neighbour was due to go on holiday the next day, but his daughter had just crashed the family car, and they could no longer go. Simon then offered the use of their family car, a Volvo estate. The neighbour thought the offer could not possibly be serious, so declined, but when pressed further, gradually realized that the offer was real. Slightly amazed, he took it up, and the next day, drove the Volvo estate off in the direction of the coast, waved off by Simon and his family.

All holiday he could not get out of his mind the generosity of his friend, for whom the car seemed something incidental to be loaned and risked, rather than something to be guarded and kept pristine, as most people did in their neighbourhood. When he returned, he couldn't help asking why Simon had done it. The answer came back that it was because he was a Christian, that he had learned that all their possessions were not really theirs at all, but God's, and were to be used generously for others as well as themselves. The neighbour was intrigued and began to ask why he had become a Christian. Simon explained the story of his own journey to faith simply. Over the next few weeks, more discussions took place, and questions arose. Simon confessed in rather an embarrassed fashion that he wasn't that good at answering them all, but that his church ran an Alpha course that gave people a chance to ask any question, and explore Christian faith for themselves. To cut a long story short, intrigued by this liberating approach to life and possessions, the neighbour eventually became a Christian.

It's a simple example, but it makes the point. All three of the elements mentioned above were present. Simon was willing to live a public Christian life, looking for practical ways of letting God's rule extend over his use of possessions as well as his use of Sunday mornings. He was willing to tell the story of his own journey to faith when called upon to do so. He was also fortunate enough to have a church that had a regular course running for those interested to discover more.

If Simon had just tried to engage his neighbour in a religious conversation, it's unlikely he would have been that interested – the desire was not there. When Christian life extends not just to church attendance, but brings the whole of a person's life under the rule of God, then it begins to provoke questions and is a much better context for evangelism. On the other hand, if Simon had lent the car, but said nothing when asked about it, his friend would have assumed he was just a particularly nice man and left it at that. To say something about the motivation that came from his faith was a risk – he couldn't tell how his neighbour would react. Yet without it, no evangelism would have happened, and his neighbour would never have been drawn to ask more about this act of reckless generosity and the faith that inspired it. If Simon had done both of these things yet not had a place to which to point his friend, where he could ask his questions and hear a good explanation of Christian faith, again it's likely that the process would not have got much further than unanswered questions and frustrated hopes.

The conditions for the growth of kingdom life are quite simple in some ways. In other ways they involve hard work and careful study. These three areas need some more exploration.

Living public Christian lives

To live publicly as a Christian requires a strong sense of Christian identity, so that you never feel you need to apologize for being a Christian. As a Christian, my primary identity lies not in my job, family background, social class or ethnic origin. There is one part of my life that supersedes all that – my life in Christ.

With a strong sense of Christian identity, Christians can be encouraged simply to be their own Christian selves in front of their neighbours and work colleagues. As they work out with their fellow believers what it means to live under the rule of God, they are to live those lives publicly, never make a secret of the fact that they are Christian, and wait to see what happens. They do not need to pressurize or quiz their non-Christian friends about their lack of belief. Replying to the simple question, 'What did you do at the weekend?' with 'I went to church' doesn't have to be followed by an evangelistic interrogation. It can be left at that, and friends can be left to figure out the connection (if there is one!) between going to church and the different set of values exhibited by this Christian in their midst. The task is primarily to get on with living a Christian life publicly. What happens will depend a lot on the circumstances. In some places it may lead to persecution. In others it will lead to evangelism.

One of the key tasks for the leadership of a local church is to work out with the rest of the members what 'life under the rule of God' means in their own particular social and geographical context. Living in wealthy suburbia, the willingness to lend a Volvo estate and not worrying or complaining if it comes back damaged is a good example. In other contexts it will be different, which is why this book or any other should be wary of prescribing too quickly what that lifestyle will be. However, this work needs to be done, and it needs to be practical and adventurous.

The next step is to encourage the public face of this style of life, both in the sense of letting it shape public behaviour as well as private habits, and also in being very open about being Christian. This may involve a few changed habits. Studies suggest that several years after conversion, most Christians will have lost most of their previous friendships. Church can be all-consuming, eating up every moment of available time, as the new eager believer is co-opted onto the outreach committee, helps run the youth club, goes to a home group, plays the drums on Sunday (with a midweek rehearsal of course), and volunteers cheerfully for the cleaning rota. The result is the rapid dwindling of wider friendships, and the loss of this public dimension of Christian life. It ends up being lived out in front of other Christians. Something Jesus said about lights and bushels comes to mind. Clergy are often worse at this than most. Using the excuse of their office (and granted, it's hard to resist the pressure in the other direction), it's a rare treat to find full-time ministers who have significant friendships with people outside the Church. Those who don't, unconsciously model to everyone else in church that it's perfectly OK to surround yourself with Christian friends and live a private Christian life.

Telling personal stories

While pre-packaged gospel outlines can seem a bit forced and fake, personal stories have an honesty and individuality that can be very powerful. If there is one way in which 'ordinary Christians' can be prepared for involvement in evangelism, surely it is by helping them identify what it means for them to be a Christian, and to be able to put that into words. In preparing churches for missions, I sometimes ask people two questions: 'How did you first become a Christian?' and 'What is the best thing for you about being a Christian?' The answers vary a great deal, but usually offer a very good clue to the heart of what that person needs to say to anyone who asks them about their faith.

Some have been Christians as long as they can remember. Some have dramatic and sudden conversion stories. For some the best thing is knowing they are completely and utterly forgiven; for others it is the delicious sense of belonging to a group of people who accept and love them; for others still it is knowing that death is nothing to be afraid of. It doesn't really matter a great deal what the answer is to these questions as long as it's honest, and it comes with a willingness to speak when the time comes. Many Christians may struggle to explain complicated ideas, but they can simply speak of their experience of Christ and life under his rule.

Providing a setting for evangelism

While many Christians will find their evangelistic ministry arising out of their living a public Christian life, and the questions arising from it, others will have real gifts in the area of explaining, persuading and answering difficult questions. Another key role in the leadership of evangelistic churches is identifying such people and enabling them to use those gifts in the context of an Alpha course, or some other type of discovery group. As we have seen, few churches grow without them, and a vital part of the pattern of evangelism explained here is the provision of a place where questions can be answered, and the heart of Christian faith can be explained. Simon needed somewhere he could point his neighbour when the questions emerged. It was his church leader's job to ensure that place was there, and that Simon knew why it was there.

Not everything in church is done for evangelistic purposes. Running a lunch club for lonely elderly people, a visiting programme for local disabled people, or lending a Volvo estate to a disconsolate neighbour – none of these are done for evangelistic effect. They are done because they express the rule of God – this is what happens when God is in charge. Yet, they all have an evangelistic dimension, as they have the potential of provoking the question, and when they are done out of Christian love and care, they often will. In this sense, everything a church does has an evangelistic dimension.

Preparing the church flowers early on a Sunday morning may seem a mundane and unspiritual activity. Yet the ministry of making the setting look attractive and colourful sends a vital message about life, colour and vigour to anyone who may happen to drop in that morning. Looking after the church lawns and gardens is not evangelism, but it does have an evangelistic dimension, as it can say a great deal about how a church looks after its small part of creation for the sake of the community around it. Pointing out simple things like this can encourage those whose gifts are not in articulate evangelism to see that their ministry is a vital part of the process of evangelism in a local church. It can also lead to a revolution in the way those tasks are fulfilled, as flower arrangers and gardeners begin to realize their place and value in the kingdom of God. When we see our ordinary work in the larger perspective of God's rule, it takes on a dignity and meaning that it lacks outside of that wider vision. When church members know how their varied ministries are related to the task of evangelism, and know that there is always somewhere they can point those who are intrigued by life under God's rule, then no matter what their gifts or ministry, it can lead to the growth of the church.

Notes

1 See Peter Brierley, *The Tide is Running Out*, London: Christian Research, 2000, p. 34, for some statistics on church decline in the UK, and pp. 84–9 for some analysis of the reasons for this, many of which point to leadership as a key issue.
2 The most penetrating and influential contemporary analysis of truth and power is that of Michel Foucault. See for example the essays in Colin Gordon, *Michel Foucault: Power/Knowledge*, New York: Harvester/Wheatsheaf, 1980.
3 John Drane, *Faith in a Changing Culture*, London: Marshall Pickering, 1997, p. 163.
4 For more on this topic, see: Ralph W. Neighbour, *Where Do We Go From Here?: A Guidebook for the Cell Group Church*, Houston, TX: Touch Publications, 1990; William A. Beckham, *The Second Reformation: Reshaping the Church of the Twentieth Century*, Houston, TX: Touch, 1995; Phil Potter, *The Challenge of Cell Church: Getting to Grips with Cell Church Values*, Oxford: Bible Reading Fellowship, 2001; Michael Green (ed.), *Church Without Walls*, Carlisle: Paternoster, 2002.
5 See Robert and Julia Banks, *The Church Comes Home*, Peabody, MA: Hendrickson, 1998.
6 Beckham, *Second Reformation*, p. 170.
7 Beckham, *Second Reformation*, p. 171.

CHAPTER 10

A theological postscript – why doesn't the New Testament mention evangelism more often?

Why doesn't the New Testament mention evangelism much? Even the most committed evangelist, reading its pages with an open mind, has to admit that its authors hardly ever urge church members to 'get out there and tell their friends about Jesus'. People like Paul, Peter and John preach wherever they go, found churches and evangelize like mad. But when they get around to writing to the 'ordinary Christians' in these churches later on, they never seem to do what you'd expect them to: urge church members to be active personal evangelists. There is a lot there about Christian doctrine, about the person and work of Christ, the cross and the resurrection. There's also quite a bit about the unity of the church, personal and corporate behaviour, relationships in families, households, civic society and the rest, but disappointingly little about evangelism *per se*.

The New Testament's silence on the subject has always been something of an embarrassment to evangelists and those of us who are keen to see an evangelistic edge to church life, and so we have either quietly ignored it or tried to get round it by devious means. When I was a student, I remember sitting in a Christian meeting in which a speaker tried to answer this very question. Why didn't the New Testament writers say much about evangelism? 'Because they assumed that everyone was doing it all the time, so they had no need to mention it!' was his answer. I wasn't convinced then and am still not now. Arguments from silence are always shaky, and in any case, were Christians then really that much better than they are today? Surely they were subject to the same shyness, fear and anxiety in speaking about their faith as we are. The earliest Christians weren't always shining examples of faith and faithfulness – just read what Paul has to say about the Galatians or the Corinthians to be reminded that those churches were as imperfect as ours!

The view from Ephesus

The letter to the Ephesians is a case in point. It paints a picture of God's design for creation from the beginning to its end, placing the Church in the centre of the frame. Yet the Greek verb *euangelizomai*, to evangelize, is not mentioned at all. As the letter has a lot to say about the Church and its pivotal place in human and divine history, you might expect it to have quite a bit to say about evangelism, but it doesn't. The nearest it gets is in Ephesians 6.19–20 (RSV), where Paul (although there is some debate, we'll assume he is the author) asks them to pray 'that utterance may be given me in opening my mouth boldly to proclaim the mystery of the gospel . . . that I may declare it boldly, as I ought to speak'. So let's take these verses as a starting point to listen carefully to what the book might be saying about the ministry of evangelism.

The mystery of the gospel

Paul is obviously quite fond of the phrase, 'the mystery of the gospel' – he uses it several times in the letter, as it seems to express something very important for him.

In chapter 3, he reminds them of his 'insight into the mystery of Christ', and explains what it is: 'This mystery is that through the gospel the Gentiles are heirs together with Israel, members together of one body, and sharers together in the promise in Christ Jesus' (Ephesians 3.4–6).

This may come as a bit of a surprise. It's probably not what most modern-day evangelists would describe as the central mystery of the gospel. Yet for Paul, the issue of getting Jews and Gentiles to meet together in one body, sharing side by side in Jesus Christ, was an essential part of the gospel, not a side issue. In fact, at another point in his career, he nearly split the Church and scuppered his own ecclesiastical career over this very point. When visiting Antioch (Galatians 2.11ff.), he was shocked to find Peter dining exclusively with Jewish Christians, refusing to eat with Gentile ones. For Paul, Peter's actions were not an unfortunate slip, much less a matter of private judgement; they struck right at the heart of the mystery of the gospel itself. So why is this such a big deal for him?

The exhibition

At the very start of the letter, Paul had explained what God has in mind for the cosmos. His secret design is 'to bring all things in heaven and on earth together under one head, even Christ' (Ephesians 1.10). All of creation is to be brought together, converging into a creative harmony. All that is destructive and evil is to be banished for ever. A divided humanity is to be reunited, and a broken creation is to be healed and reordered under Christ its head. Paul can hardly be accused of limited vision! The view from Ephesus ranges far and wide over time and eternity. Yet of course it needs to come down to earth. Where is the evidence for this vision? How do we know it isn't a pipe dream, a grand, inspiring but ultimately empty vision?

Further on in Ephesians 3, the answer comes: 'now, *through the church*, the manifold wisdom of God should be made known to the rulers and authorities in the heavenly realms, according to his eternal purpose which he accomplished in Christ Jesus our Lord' (Ephesians 3.10–11).

God wants to show off his wisdom and craft to the rest of the cosmos. God the divine artist wants to hold an exhibition of such beauty and power and wisdom that anyone who looks on, whether they come from earth or heaven, will be overcome with wonder and awe. It is to be a display of his 'manifold' (the word can be otherwise translated as 'varied' or 'variegated') wisdom.

The trailer

And this is where the Jew–Gentile issue comes in. For Paul, the hard evidence that God will one day bring all things together under Christ is found in these small Christian communities scattered around the Roman Empire, which are busy uniting Gentile and Jew, freemen and slaves, women and men. This is, if you like, the sneak preview of the exhibition, the trailer for the main feature yet to be shown.

Since the coming of Jesus Christ, the world is a different place. A lavish array of good, gracious gifts have descended upon humanity through the death of Christ – life through death, redemption, the forgiveness of sins and reconciliation with God. And now also, the Gentiles, who once were distant strangers to God's covenant people the Jews, have been brought near (Ephesians 2.13).

The law, which once marked off God's people Israel from the rest, has now been abolished (Ephesians 2.15), in the sense that it is no longer the distinguishing mark of the people of God. No longer are God's people recognizable as those who are circumcised, keep food laws and ritual purity. Instead, they are those who believe in Jesus the Messiah, in whom God's kingdom has come.[1]

The uniting of Jew and Gentile was one of the signs given in the Old Testament that the end had come, that God had finally become king.[2] It's not surprising, therefore, that if Jesus thought that God's kingdom was coming through his own death and resurrection, and Paul came to believe him, then Paul would draw the inevitable conclusion. If God's kingdom has come, and the promised new age has now broken into human history, now is the time for Jew and Gentile to be drawn together under Christ, just as the Old Testament had said should one day happen.

The Church of Jesus Christ has therefore become for Paul the place where the promised reconciliation takes place. It is the place where everything that wants to be is brought together under Christ. A broken and divided creation is finally reconciled to itself and to God in the body of Christ. In the light of all this, perhaps it begins to dawn on us why Paul gets so excited about the idea of Gentiles coming to church, sitting next to Jews, and handing them the communion cup. Here is the 'hard evidence' of his grand exhilarating vision.

The home

Even more than this, for Paul, the Church also becomes the dwelling place for God on earth (Ephesians 2.22). Jews were familiar with the idea that God lived in the temple in Jerusalem. Pagan Gentiles were familiar with gods dwelling in the temples of their own cult. Paul thought differently – God has now set up home in the

Church of Jesus Christ. It is an outrageous, audacious claim, to suggest that if you wanted to find God in Ephesus, you would need to find the small, socially mixed bunch of people who were worshipping Jesus Christ. The Church was of course anything but a grand institution with cathedrals, bishops and friends in high places. You could have easily spent a whole week in Ephesus, Corinth or Philippi and never have come across it at all. Nevertheless, these tiny gatherings of Christians were for Paul, 'a dwelling in which God lives by his Spirit'. God is the householder, and all kinds of different people live in his house: Jewish slaves, Gentile artisans, women merchants and noisy children. He owns, shares and dwells in his own house.

The Church is therefore both the foretaste of the coming reconciled world, and the dwelling place of God on earth. The calling of Gentiles into God's people is a central part of Paul's ministry because their presence alongside Jews expresses God's varied, manifold wisdom. It is vital that this community is open to all peoples because this was the foretaste of the reconciliation of all things in Christ at the end of the ages. It was essential for Paul that this community was not monochrome, but variegated. The community had to welcome not only rich, Jewish and socially respectable people but also Gentiles, slaves, women, young and old. Only so could it reflect God's intention to bring together God's divided creation, and display his 'manifold wisdom'. Church is a place where that coming kingdom can be tasted and experienced. The result is the creation of a new kind of person altogether. Out of the ancient division of humankind into Jew and Gentile, God is now creating 'a new humanity' (see Ephesians 2.15), a new kind of person, marked not by ethnic or social identity, but by faith in Christ and a whole new set of behavioural characteristics.

A theological postscript

Preparing the ground

Before describing what this new kind of person looks like, Paul lays the foundations, spelling out the ingredients needed if this kind of reconciled community is to survive and thrive. When Paul gets round to praying for the Ephesian Christians in 3.14–21, he doesn't pray primarily for their evangelism but for their growth in spirit, that Christ may dwell in their hearts, that they may have the capacity to take in the sheer volume of the love of Christ, and most staggering of all, that they will be 'filled to the brim with the fullness of God'.

Then he depicts the kind of characteristics they will need to cultivate if this vision of a reconciled community is to work (Ephesians 4.2–3). They aren't very exciting qualities (humility, patience, putting up with one another out of love) but they are precisely the kind of things you need if you are going to enable very different people, who would normally come to blows within minutes, to get on together.

Then there are the gifts God has given to bring this vision to reality (Ephesians 4.7–16). Apostles plant churches, prophets speak God's words to them, evangelists add new people to those churches, pastors put into practice God's care for his people, teachers keep reminding them of Jesus and the big vision of God's design and, using these as his tools, God's Spirit transforms Christians into people eager to serve, discerning in their faith, speaking truth gently and with love, all under Christ the Head, the King, under whose rule they live.

The marks of the new humanity

As these people begin to do their work, a new kind of person emerges, different from the old type, which was

The Provocative Church

'darkened in . . . understanding and separated from the life of God' (Ephesians 4.18). This is a community that lives by different rules, assumptions and norms from the rest of human society, and Paul examines four very practical aspects of life as examples of the difference.

First, there is new *community*. Here, the bottom line is truthfulness, transparency and honesty (Ephesians 4.25). Yes, it is sometimes painful to be truthful, but members of this new community pledge to be honest and straightforward with one another. Here, anger is dealt with quickly, and it is not allowed to fester, lest it turn into a stone-cold bitterness (4.26–27). Burglars don't just stop stealing; they start giving. They find themselves transformed into part of the solution rather than the problem of a broken world – they change from parasites on society to agents of social improvement as they learn to give generously to those in need (4.28). There is a determination here not to undermine or demean others, but instead to use words positively, to encourage, affirm and bless (4.29). People learn the skill of forgiveness by learning first how much they have been forgiven by God, and how much that pardon cost (4.32).

The next area to be transformed is that of *desire*, the sex, drugs and rock 'n' roll of the first century. In this new humanity, people renounce from the very start a life of self-gratification (Ephesians 4.17–19). It may be the basic rule of life outside but here, they understand how destructive it is of human community, and so it is left behind. Sexual selfishness and exploitation is out of the question – it is not even mentioned. Sex is received as a good and pleasurable gift for which satisfied thanks is given, but it no longer dominates and damages relationships (5.3–4). God has created us to experience the thrill of ecstasy and the 'buzz' of heightened consciousness. Yet these are to be found in pouring out the soul in heartfelt

166

wonder and adoration of this fascinating and good God, rather than from the abuse of alcohol, which leads to uncontrolled abuse, or a drug-induced frenzy (5.18–20). The next area concerns *family* life. Here the key theme is mutual submission, not competition. Where family is so often a place of conflict and pain, in this community, mutual submission leads to a harmony in variety. Differences between men and women are acknowledged, yet hierarchical domination is out of order. Husbands and wives are helped to respect one another rather than take one another for granted. The kind of love Christ showed to the Church (rather than sexual desire or authoritarian power) is to be the bond that holds their marriages together (Ephesians 5.21–33). Children are taught the wisdom of obedience; parents learn patience and self-control with their children.

Finally, there is the sphere of *work*. Here, slaves (or employees in our terms) are encouraged to imagine themselves working under Jesus Christ, and taught to give the same respect and trust to their masters or managers as they would to him (Ephesians 6.5–8). Clock-watching or working hard when the boss is looking and slacking when he's out of the room is out of the question. Work is undertaken not primarily for financial gain, or even job satisfaction; instead, it is done as an act of worship to God, and looking to him for any sense of reward. Masters and managers themselves are to know their limitations. They do not own their employees, nor do they have the power of life or death over them. Knowing they are accountable not to a board of directors but to God himself is to govern their own conduct at work. Any sense that God favours bosses over workers, the successful over the unsuccessful, the wealthy over the underpaid, is unthinkable. God's love extends to all exactly the same. So employers are to treat their employees as objects of God's love and favour, deserving of dignity and honour.

Here is a snapshot of the new kind of humanity God is creating out of the old. It is the goal of the journey, a practical image of holiness in real life which the church as a community tries to cultivate in the life of each person in it, and in its own corporate life.

Back to evangelism

So, to return to our original question, why doesn't Ephesians (and the rest of the New Testament) mention evangelism more often?

The answer is surely that the Church's first task is to be what it is meant to be, to display the wisdom of God to whoever looks in from the outside. This new community is called to demonstrate, by the distinctiveness of its life and the harmony created among very different people, God's variegated wisdom. The task is to learn to live the Christian life before we talk about it; to walk the walk, before we talk the talk. God has chosen to work out his will for the world not through a bunch of individuals being sent out to persuade others to believe in him, but by creating a new community made up of very different people, giving them his Spirit who enables them to live together in unity, to develop a new way of life and to live this way of life publicly.

Evangelism then finds its place within this context. Even though it isn't highlighted as the highest priority of every Christian, evangelists are still key figures within the local church. The role of the evangelist (Paul himself is a prime example) is to articulate on behalf of the rest of the community the invitation to come under God's rule, to become part of this new humanity, to join in what God is doing. That's why Paul asks them to pray for him, that he will 'fearlessly make known the mystery of the gospel', even though it has landed him in prison. He calls the evangelists in Ephesus to do the same – there is no sense that only apostles are entrusted with this task – as he fully expects individuals within the local church to be identified as gifted in evangelism (Ephesians 4.11).

Now that may not sound much like your local church (nor mine either, come to that). Yet we often under-estimate the power of the work of God's Spirit among us. Dietrich Bonhoeffer reminds us:

> Only God knows the real state of our fellowship, of our sanctification. What may appear weak and trifling to us may appear great and glorious to God . . . Christian brotherhood is not an ideal which we must realize; it is rather a reality created by God in Christ in which we may participate.[3]

It's a salutary reminder, in case we are tempted to try too hard! What may seem ordinary to us can seem extraordinary to others, and the business of inviting people into the fellowship that Christians share with God is really quite simple. From his careful research, John Finney reminds us that 'for most people, the cor-porate life of church is a vital element in the process of becoming a Christian, and for about a quarter it is the vital factor'.[4] And as a result he suggests: 'Training in evangelism should mention that one of the simplest and most effective forms of evangelism is "would you like to come to church with me next Sunday?" '[5]

He's talking here about real, ordinary churches, full of sinners struggling to manage work, families, temptations and making ends meet. Yet at the same time, churches where there is a genuine sense that God is slowly chang-ing people into this new kind of person which Paul describes in Ephesians. It's surprising how attractive ordinary churches can be.

By and large, the letter to the Ephesians doesn't tell Christians to make a priority of getting out there and evangelizing. It does tell them to love each other, to learn a new way of relating in families and at work, to gain freedom from damaging obsessions, and a healthy scepticism towards the idols of the age. It tells them to develop a completely new way of living. That is the priority. And when that begins to happen, the word of the evangelist, or even the simple recounting of a personal journey to faith, rings true because it connects with the reality experienced among God's people.

Notes

1 The notion of the 'abolition of the law' in Ephesians is a controversial issue and part of a much wider discussion of Paul's understanding of the place of the Torah after Christ. For a discussion of these issues, the reader is directed to the helpful discussion in Andrew T. Lincoln, *Ephesians*, Word Biblical Commentary, Dallas, TX: Word, 1990, pp. 139–46.
2 See for example Isaiah 2.2–4 and Micah 4.1–4.
3 Dietrich Bonhoeffer, *Life Together*, London: SCM, 1954, p. 18.
4 John Finney, *Finding Faith Today: How Does It Happen?*, Swindon: BFBS, 1992, p. 43.
5 Finney, *Finding Faith*, p. 79.

Study guide

—●—

This Study guide includes ten studies, one for each chapter. Groups with less time (Lent groups, for example) might just take the studies for Chapters 1, 3, 5, 8 and 10. The studies will work best if members have read the relevant chapter beforehand. A church might consider combining these group studies with a sermon series on the topics of the book.

1 Evangelism that works and evangelism that doesn't

Read Acts 2.42–47.

In the first chapter we are introduced to two people, John Diamond and Derek Draper, who have very different reactions to Christianity.

Spend a few moments thinking about your own journey of faith:

1 What first attracted you to Christianity?
2 What most excites you about being a Christian today?
3 If someone asked you why you attend your church what would you say?
4 Now think about someone you know well who is clearly not interested in Christianity. Think about what they enjoy and what you enjoy about that person. Are they not interested in God or not interested in the Church, or both? Why do you think they are not interested?

5 Would you feel comfortable asking them to the church in Acts 2? Would you feel comfortable inviting them to your church? If so, why? If not, why not?

6 What would it take for them to become genuinely interested?

7 Finish by discussing this question (p. 13): 'Is our church just another little club for like-minded people who happen to enjoy singing, religious emotion and sermons? Or is there anything in the life or worship of our church that would make an outsider looking in want to have what we have?'

2 Should we be doing this?

Read Romans 10.8–15.

1 What images come to mind when you hear the word 'evangelism' or 'evangelist'? Are they positive or negative?

2 Chapter 2 begins with an analysis of the pluralist/ postmodern context in which we live (pp. 17–19). From your observations and discussion above do you agree with the description of our culture today? What would you add?

3 Do you or your church speak much about the kingdom of God? What do you understand by the phrase?

4 Share your reaction to the story of Robin Hood (pp. 28f) as an example of the Church and the kingdom of God. What do you find helpful about the picture?

5 Look again at the attitudes Jacques Ellul suggests Christians need to have if they are to relate rightly to the world around them (pp. 20–6). How might your church help you develop a 'distinctive or alternative way [of life] to the ways of life on offer in the wider culture' (p. 24)? Can you begin to think what such a way of life might look like?

Study guide

3 The king, the kingdom and the Book

Read Matthew 13.24–35.

1 Look at Matthew 13.24–35. How would you describe the kingdom of God in one or two sentences?
2 Spend time discussing what it means to claim 'Jesus is Lord'. How would you explain this claim to someone who had never heard about Jesus before?
3 'Kings' and 'kingdom' are not terms we use very often today, and sometimes carry unpopular connotations of hierarchy and authority. Can you think of other words or concepts to convey the idea of Jesus' lordship and rule today (e.g. 'master', 'life coach', 'guide')?
4 'Loyalty to Jesus . . . meant rejecting the lordship of other claimants to that title' (p. 52). What are the idols which people in your area, or your friends, tend to worship? (Wealth? Popularity? Success? Power? Comfort? Fame?) How might you show your rejection of those idols?
5 What might your local community or workplace look like if God was in charge and had his way? What would be different?
6 How might your church demonstrate these things in practical ways?

4 The kingdom, the Church and evangelism

Read Mark 1.14–20.

1 Which of the ten 'theses' did you find most surprising or challenging and why?
Thesis 1: The gospel centres on the lordship of Christ.
2 Words like 'repentance' are not used much today. How would you explain to someone who is not a regular churchgoer what repentance means?

3 What kind of 'normal' behaviour among your friends would need to change if they were to 'live as if it were true that Jesus is Lord'?

Thesis 3: The community of Jesus has the task of bearing witness to his rightful rule.

4 Look back at the temple picture on p. 44 and note the way different groups are excluded.

Think of your own church. Are there areas where people are excluded in general or during worship, e.g. children, lay people, the disabled? Is that right or wrong?

5 Look back at the key features of the kingdom from pp. 50–2. In what ways are these features of openness, difference, action and rejection features of your local church community? Try to identify examples from the life of your church for each of these key features.

Thesis 9: Evangelism can never stand alone.

6 Is it more important to show the good news of Jesus by our actions or to tell others about Jesus? Where does the emphasis lie in your church? Does it get the balance right?

7 Are there places or times when you would feel uncomfortable speaking about your faith? If yes, is this because it would be inappropriate or because you would just feel uncomfortable?

5 'Evangelism makes me feel guilty'

Read 1 Peter 3.8–18.

1 How does the thought of 'doing' evangelism make you feel? E.g. guilty, excited, terrified, bored, frustrated?

2 Do you consider you have the resources and gifts for evangelism? If yes, what might they be? If no, what do you think these gifts and resources should be and who might have them?

Study guide

3 Is it possible to stress evangelism too much? If so, why? If not, why not?
4 Look at 1 Peter 3.15. Try to recall a time when someone asked you about your faith, or the fact that you go to church. What was it that provoked them to ask the question? Was it something you said or did?
5 Explore some possible reasons why people might *not* ask such questions about Christians today.
6 On pp. 76–8 are some examples of ways in which Christian action and behaviour provoked questions from others. Do you know other examples of people being 'provoked' in such a way? These may be historical examples or people you know personally.
7 The chapter goes on to suggest some small practical acts of love, goodness and generosity (p. 81). Spend a few moments thinking about some similar ways in which you could engage in small practical acts this coming week which demonstrate God's freely given love for his creation.

6 Is my church worth going to?

Read John 3.1–15.
1 Would you describe your coming to faith as a sudden conversion or a gradual process?
2 In this chapter a distinction is drawn between 'regeneration' and 'transformation' (pp. 90f). Do you find the distinction helpful? Which one do you and your church tend to emphasize more?
3 Look at John 3.1–15 and its language of being 'born again'. What is helpful or unhelpful about this image? The term 'born again' often has negative connotations for people outside the Church. How else would you describe what Jesus is talking about here?

175

4 'Faith is not a thing which one "loses", we merely cease to shape our lives by it' (p. 98). Do you agree with this statement? Have there been times when this has been true for you? Do you know others whom this has happened to? Why has it happened?

5 Would you describe your church community as healthy?

6 What 'healthy' qualities in your church's life excite you enough to want to invite others to share in it?

7 What is there in your life or the life of your church which 'remains to be converted'?

7 Transforming communities

Read Colossians 1.15–20.

1 Do you find it easier to think of Jesus in terms of his humanity or divinity? Why?

2 Look at 2 Peter 1.2–9. 'The more like God we become, the more human we become, not less' (p. 109). Is this true? In what ways is it appropriate to become like God? Are there ways in which it is inappropriate?

3 This chapter suggests that church communities need to have an agenda for change in the wider community. What would the wider community miss if your church was no longer there?

4 What 'marks of the kingdom', or signs of the rule of Christ, do people in your community need to see or experience most of all? (Peace? Belonging? Purpose? Hope? Love? Joy? Forgiveness? Rest?) Try to focus on one or two main ones.

5 Thinking of Galatians 5.22–23, can you think of gestures, programmes or lifestyle choices which you or your church might adopt, which would express the 'marks of the kingdom' you identified in question 4?

Study guide

8 How to spot an evangelistic church

Read 1 Corinthians 14.23–28.
The study focuses on the five areas of relationship identified on p. 122. Use the table below and mark your church on each of the five areas by circling a number from 1 to 10 according to how well you think the church does.

Relationship	Very poor								Very good
With God – Adoration	1 2 3 4 5 6 7 8 9 10								
With others – Belonging	1 2 3 4 5 6 7 8 9 10								
With creation – Compassion	1 2 3 4 5 6 7 8 9 10								
With ourselves – Discipleship	1 2 3 4 5 6 7 8 9 10								
With words – Evangelism	1 2 3 4 5 6 7 8 9 10								

Compare responses to the exercise above (in a group setting, you might like to work out an average 'score' for each section). In which areas does your church do well? Where does your church score badly?

In the following section, start with those areas where you feel your church is not doing so well and work towards those where it is quite strong, depending on how much time you have.

1 Adoration
What aspects of your church's public worship have most helped you to sense the presence and reality of God?

Look at 1 Corinthians 14.23–26. Do you find this an attractive picture of church worship and if so what is it that attracts you?

In what ways can you help foster in your church an expectation of worship that is dynamic and provocative?

2 *Belonging*
Would you describe your church as one where people are expected to observe and receive or to participate and contribute?

Spend a few moments picturing the people in your church. How diverse is your church community (e.g. age, background, culture, ethnicity)? Does the church reflect the wider local community? If not, what are the reasons for this and how might these factors be overcome?

How could your church help to develop more participation, interaction and growth in relationships? What part can you play in this?

3 *Compassion*
Spend a few moments recalling some of Jesus' miracles. In what ways did the miracles act as signs of the restoration of creation? In what ways does your church demonstrate God's love for his creation? What are some of the things that need healing in your local community? What further practical responses might you and the church make to set up signs of the kingdom? (Some examples are given on p. 134. Try to be imaginative, practical and realistic in your response.)

4 *Discipleship*
What are the areas of your life and the lives of others in your church where you would like help in developing a distinctive Christian way of life?

How might your church, or the churches in your area, offer such help? (For instance, would a course like the one described on pp. 135–6 help? Would it be possible?

What kind of things might it address which are key issues for you and your locality?)

5 Evangelism
Does your church provide a place for searchers to explore what it means to be a Christian? How effective is it, and how might it be made more effective?
Could you explain what it means to you to be a Christian? Could you 'give the reason for the hope that you have' (1 Peter 3.15)? Try doing so to each other in the group.
How might your church help you become better at explaining and defending your faith to others?

9 Leading evangelistic churches

Read 1 Corinthians 3.5–9.
1 How helpful is the image of the gardener in thinking about leadership (pp. 143ff)? What are the strengths or weaknesses of this image?
2 What is the primary focus of the home groups/study groups in your church? (See pp. 147–50.) Does this need to change?
3 Are you attracted to the 'cell church' model described in this chapter? What are the strengths of this model? What are the potential problems? What would be the role and responsibilities of the vicar/minister in a church organized like this?
4 Who are the 'natural' evangelists in your church? What are the qualities and gifts that mark them out for this ministry? How does the church support them in using this gift?
5 How can you constructively help and develop the leadership of your church, including your vicar/ minister, other staff, group leaders, etc.?

10 A theological postscript

Read the book of Ephesians (try and do it in one go).

1 Why do you think Paul speaks of the gospel as a 'mystery' or 'secret'?

2 Look up Ephesians 2.11–22 and 3.4–6. 'The uniting of Jew and Gentile was one of the signs given in the Old Testament that the end had come, that God had finally become king.' Thinking of both your own local area and the wider world, what groups of people today, if brought together in unity under Christ, would be a powerful sign of the kingdom?

3 Look at Ephesians 1.9–10. Try to flesh out what this vision of 'all things in heaven and on earth together under . . . Christ' would look like.

4 Look at Ephesians 4.17—6.9. The Church is to be a community that is marked by a distinctive way of life. Four aspects of life are identified: community, desire, family, work. Choose one of these areas and identify one practical thing you can do during this next week to demonstrate life under the rule of God in that area.

5 Spend the remainder of this study together identifying the key issues and challenges that have arisen for you and your church as a result of studying this book.

References and further reading

————◄●►————

William J. Abraham, *The Logic of Evangelism*, London: Hodder, 1989.
(A useful theology of evangelism written from the American context)

Robert and Julia Banks, *The Church Comes Home*, Peabody, MA: Hendrickson, 1998.
(A good guide to home churches)

William A. Beckham, *The Second Reformation: Reshaping the Church of the Twentieth Century*, Houston, TX: Touch, 1995.
(One of the key books on cell church)

Walter Brueggemann, *Biblical Perspectives on Evangelism: Living in a Three-Storied Universe*, Nashville, TN: Abingdon Press, 1993.
(A thoughtful essay on evangelism through the eyes of some biblical themes)

John Drane, *Faith in a Changing Culture*, London: Marshall Pickering, 1997.
(A perceptive look at the Church in the context of the post-modern spiritual search)

Jacques Ellul, *The Presence of the Kingdom*, 2nd ed., Colorado Springs, CO: Helmers & Howard, 1989.
(First written in 1948, a prophetic account of the place of the Church in modern society)

Michael Green (ed.), *Church Without Walls*, Carlisle: Paternoster, 2002.
(A collection of essays from different parts of the world on the cell church phenomenon)

Lesslie Newbigin, *Foolishness to the Greeks: The Gospel and Western Culture*, London: SPCK, 1986.
(An analysis of Western culture as a missionary challenge)

181

References and further reading

Lesslie Newbigin, *The Gospel in a Pluralist Society*, London: SPCK, 1989.
(Fascinating series of chapters on the gospel, mission, pluralism, other faiths, etc.)

Phil Potter, *The Challenge of Cell Church*, Oxford: Bible Reading Fellowship, 2001.
(Up-to-date and practical guide to the principles of cell church)

Graham Tomlin, 'Evangelicalism and Evangelism', in *Evangelical Anglicans: Their Role and Influence in the Church Today*, ed. R. T. France and A. E. McGrath, London: SPCK, 1993, pp. 82–95.
(An essay on the relationship between evangelicalism, Anglicanism and evangelism)

Graham Tomlin, *Spiritual Fitness: Christian Character in a Consumer Culture*, London: Continuum, 2006.
(Exploring the analogy between churches and gyms as places for personal transformation)

Rick Warren, *The Purpose Driven Church: Growth without Compromising Your Message and Mission*, Grand Rapids, MI: Zondervan, 1995.
(Punchy and practical account of principles of growing churches)

Robert Warren, *Being Human, Being Church*, London: Marshall Pickering, 1995.
(Important and stimulating book from an authority in the area of new patterns of church life)

N. T. Wright, *Jesus and the Victory of God*, London: SPCK, 1996.
(Crucial book on Jesus in his historical context and particularly the role of the kingdom of God in his life and teaching)

Index

CPSIA information can be obtained at www.ICGtesting.com
Printed in the USA
LVOW05s1439161014

409092LV00015B/624/P